HOW TO DEAL WITH
ADVERSITY

Also by Christopher Hamilton

Living Philosophy

Middle Age

HOW TO DEAL WITH ADVERSITY

Christopher Hamilton

PICADOR

New York

www.picadorusa.com
www.twitter.com/picadorusa • www.facebook.com/picadorusa
picadorbookroom.tumblr.com

Picador® is a U.S. registered trademark and is used by St. Martin's Press under license from Pan Books Limited.

For book club information, please visit www.facebook.com/picadorbookclub or e-mail marketing@picadorusa.com.

Designed by Steven Seighman

Library of Congress Cataloging-in-Publication Data is available upon request.

The photographic credits on page 205 constitute an extension of this copyright page.

ISBN 978-1-250-05900-0 (trade paperback)
ISBN 978-1-250-05901-7 (e-book)

Picador books may be purchased for educational, business, or promotional use. For information on bulk purchases, please contact Macmillan Corporate and Premium Sales Department at 1-800-221-7945, extension 5442, or write specialmarkets@macmillan.com.

Originally published in Great Britain by Macmillan, an imprint of Pan Macmillan, a division of Macmillan Publishers Limited.

First U.S. Edition: September 2014

10 9 8 7 6 5 4 3 2 1

Do not think that the person who seeks to console you lives untroubled and in accord with the simple and quiet words that sometimes help you. His life has much hardship and sadness, and remains far behind yours. If it were otherwise, he could never have found those words.

—R.M. Rilke, Letter to Franz Kappus, 12 August 1904

Contents

HOW TO DEAL WITH ADVERSITY

Introduction

The Roots of Adversity and the Nature of this Book

Everyone knows that life contains many adversities: we all experience loss, failure, disappointment, waste and pain in various different forms
and ways. This is so obviously the case that we
rarely reflect on why things are like this. But if
we want to understand how we might respond
constructively to adversity we would do well to
start by thinking about why there is adversity
in human life at all. Adversity is, I shall suggest, inevitable. There is nothing we can do to
escape it wholly. But that, far from being a negative thought, is immensely liberating, because
it allows us to gain a realistic perspective on
ourselves and on what we can really do to make
sense of, and turn to account, the adversity we
experience in life.

Limited Resources

We who live in the developed world are extremely fortunate. In many ways, we live in a world of plenty and of opportunity. We do not, in general, have to worry about the availability of food and shelter, of medical services and of educational opportunities, though the absurdities of how we organize things ensure that such resources are much more unequally distributed than they might be. Nonetheless, we do not live in a world of limitless resources and human beings are normally manifestly in competition with each other for them – concrete resources like income and property, but also more intangible resources, such as fame, reputation, status and so on. We see such competition in the job or housing market, for example, and in our desire for career advancement. Further, we are extremely physically vulnerable creatures, whose bodies are very easily damaged. We often fail to acknowledge this, even though we know it, because, in general, we experience much better health than any human beings in history. But a visit to your local A&E department will remind you just how vulnerable the human body is.

For these reasons, we naturally seek for ourselves, and for those about whom we care, the best
possible conditions of security. We all seek to shore
up our position in the world, and, although different individuals conceive of safety and security in
somewhat different ways, our desire and need for
them inevitably mean that we clash with others, because we are seeking pretty much the same things
as others, under conditions of limited resources. In
other words, we come up against adversity.

But human beings are not just physically
vulnerable; they are deeply psychologically vulnerable as well. This vulnerability comes about
partly because human desires and needs are potentially limitless, in the sense that they feed off
each other and the world around them in such
a way that human beings always seek more –
more of what they have already, or more of
something new. There are, in my view, reasons
deep within human psychology why this is so.
In particular, three ideas from the writings of
Samuel Johnson seem to me to be especially
useful in understanding this: the hunger of the
imagination; the vacuity of life; and the craving
for novelty.

The Hunger of the Imagination

The human mind, Johnson pointed out, is not a passive recipient of information from the outside. It does not neutrally register what is going on out there. On the contrary, it is an active force with a life of its own, energetic, febrile, forever in motion, like a kind of unruly or disruptive creature. It is intolerant of limitation and restraint, and seeks to expend itself. It lives very largely in the past and the future, reflecting on what has been and propelling itself into potential plans, projects, ambitions and aims. It is, in short, hungry.

This hunger is expressed in the workings of the imagination. It is because we are imaginative creatures that we can construct ideas and images of what the future might be like, formulate plans, initiate change and so on. *We can see how things could be different*, and, in our hunger, we reach out to make things correspond to the image we have: it might be that we want to buy something, or travel somewhere, or visit a friend, or learn something new, or change career – and so on, in countless ways. But because the mind is so hungry we find that once we achieve our goal we remain hungry: we want more of the same, or something different – or, paradoxically, both. This is why Plato saw human beings as like leaky buckets: pour the water in and, rather than staying put, it will flow out of the bottom. We can never be 'full', in this sense, more than momentarily. Other thinkers have followed Plato, changing the metaphor, seeing us as on a treadmill of desire, forever turning round and never coming to a halt.

Of course, all this has a positive side: we are able to mould the future in a way that other animals cannot, and we can secure ourselves in various ways against troubles and difficulties. But the profoundly disturbing aspect of the hunger of the imagination is that the experience of desire is always potentially traumatic: we *have* desires, but we are also *caught up in* them. They can pull us and tempt us in all kinds of ways, and can seem alien to us when they do so. They are ours; but we are also theirs.

Moreover, the hunger of the imagination is the source of many negative emotions and dispositions. For the imagination is the root of our capacity to compare ourselves with others, and, when we do so, we often suppose that they have something, or some things, that we do not have. This can give rise to envy, for example, or greed –

emotions unpleasant to have in themselves and also highly likely to lead to various conflicts with others.

The Vacuity of Life

Because human beings are so hungry, they experience a kind of emptiness at the centre of their existence – just as they experience an emptiness in the stomach when they are hungry for food. Johnson called this 'the vacuity of life'. Of course, individuals differ in how susceptible they are to such emptiness in psychological terms, and in how they cope with it, but we are all to a greater or lesser extent restless, constantly seeking to fill up our lives. The French philosopher Blaise Pascal famously expressed this by saying that the reason human beings are miserable is that they cannot remain quietly alone in a room. If they try to do this, they grasp acutely the vacuity of life, a sense of themselves as empty containers that cannot bear their own emptiness. Hence we crave distraction all the time. We need to fill up our time. From a very bleak perspective – Pascal's, for example – *all* human activity is basically a form of distraction, an attempt to rid ourselves of a feeling of emptiness. But even if we do not see things in this way, it can hardly be denied that very many human activities are forms of distraction in Pascal's sense.

Probably the best example of this self-distraction in the modern age is the use we often make of the technology by which we are surrounded – television, film, the Internet, mobile phones and so on. Despite its usefulness in many contexts, this technology is immensely distracting. It fills up what would otherwise be empty time – that is, the sense of emptiness we experience – and then becomes an end in itself. This is just a way of saying that such technologies are immensely addictive. I see this, for example, in the case of my students, who invariably check their mobile phones for messages and calls as soon as the class has finished. Such technology gives them a sense of never being alone, of never having to face their emptiness. But that is certainly in large part an illusion.

In any case, we distract ourselves in many ways, and it may be that the problems of contemporary societies – drug and alcohol addiction, gambling, obesity, pornography and so on – are really attempts to fill the vacuity that haunts us.

Another way of putting this is to say that the world is indifferent to us. To become addicted to something is to seek to wrest something from the world, to make it respond to us, to strip it of its indifference. This is why those who are truly addicted to something feel, when indulging the addiction, that the world is *theirs*. But, of course, when the moment has passed, they feel even more acutely the indifference of the world – which feeds the addiction. We are not all addicts. But human beings are deeply addictive creatures. That is one manifestation of their need for distraction to fill themselves up.

We all of us have to *do* something with our time, and part of the problem of human life is finding worthy things to do – things that do not involve the expenditure of energy for its own sake, but rather are constructive, or deepening, or nourishing. If you have ever rid yourself of a few hours by surfing the Internet without even really realizing that this is what you were doing, and, at the end, could not much remember what you saw or honestly say that you found anything much worth thinking about – then you know exactly what I am talking about. And you also know what Pascal was seeking to express in speaking of human beings' need for distraction.

The Craving for Novelty

Because we long to fill ourselves up, psychologically and spiritually, one of the things that haunts the human mind is boredom. Boredom is, at least in one of its forms, an unbearable sense of vacuity; it is the psychological manifestation of the sense of the vacuity of life. And one way in which we seek to evade boredom is by seeking out that which is new. We are afflicted, Johnson noted, by a craving for novelty. The French philosopher Albert Camus said that man can get used to anything. That may be true. But it is also true, and well known, that we can become bored by anything that at the outset we welcomed. In our age, the place where we see this most clearly is the consumerist market, where so much of what is bought is acquired not because what it replaces has worn out or become unusable, but simply because it has become familiar – in other words, we are bored by it. 'Fashion' is one term by which we dignify this aspect of our lives.

Psychological Mess

What all that adds up to is that human beings are deeply conflicted both within themselves and with others. They are psychologically messy in the ways I have sought to describe, and this generates conflict within and without – that is, *intrasubjective* and *intersubjective* conflict. Pained by a sense of emptiness, we inevitably clash with others as we seek the means to assuage our suffering.

I am saying nothing new: it has been said countless times since human beings started to think about the kinds of creatures they are. The great religions took these facts of the human condition deeply seriously, and sought ways in which their adherents might cope with and make sense of their suffering. Buddhism, for example, elaborated techniques of meditation and mindfulness, practices aimed at enabling us to learn to accept and thrive on the emptiness at the centre of human experience. Christianity, whose name for the restless condition I have described is 'original sin', did the same with prayer, which, in its best forms, has a purificatory function, and suggested that human beings can only finally achieve peace in the beatific vision of God after death, intimations of which are, nonetheless, available to us here in this world. One reason why many people in the modern age feel themselves to be spiritually bereft is that they can no longer really believe in the solutions such religions offer – this is part of what the German philosopher Friedrich Nietzsche meant by 'the death of God' – but the needs to which these religions ministered have not gone away.

Ontological Misfits

Because human beings know that they are psychologically messy, they devise techniques to seek to escape their condition as such. They invent ideals, seeking to transcend themselves. Christianity was one of the main such ideals in the West – and still is, for plenty of people – yet for many it is now unbelievable. But there are many other ideals: personal, ethical, political, aesthetic and so on. The basic distinction at work in an ideal is between how the world *is* and how it *ought to be*. And because we are part of the world, we subject ourselves to the kind of scrutiny in question: we *are* as we are, but seek to be what we *ought to be*, however we may conceive that.

But what this means is that *we are seeking to escape our own condition, to transcend ourselves.* Hence we can say: it is the nature of human beings to seek to escape their own condition, to long to be something else. This does not mean that all human beings are like this all the time, but it is to say that it is a feature of our fundamental, or ontological, condition: that is the kind of creature we are.

We are at odds with ourselves, and this is one of the things that distinguishes us from the other animals and why we can sometimes envy them their ability simply to be at home in the world. Traditionally, the view I am exploring has been expressed by saying that human beings are neither beasts nor angels, both of which are at peace with themselves, whilst we are not. We are *ontological misfits.* We are not at home in the world. And in my view that explains, in large part, why it is that human history is such a relentless, monstrous scene of suffering inflicted by human beings on themselves and each other: we flail around in our own wretched confusions, and as we do so we wound ourselves and those around us. In our attempts to escape our condition, to find something solid on which to rely, to make ourselves the stable thing we need, we seek to dominate ourselves and others, seek to gain control of things, and, in doing this, we invariably make things worse all round.

All well and good, you might say. If it is the nature of human beings to wish to escape their condition as human beings, and if this generates such adversity, then clearly what we need to do is to stop doing that and to accept ourselves in all our humanity. But that will not work since, obviously enough, to accept one's nature as a human being *just is* to accept that it is one's nature to seek to escape that. So either way is unsatisfactory: if you accept yourself, you will accept your longing to escape your condition, and therefore seek to do so; if you do not accept your condition as a human being then, similarly, you will seek to escape your condition. Either way, you are caught.

As I say, different individuals manifest these ontological tendencies to different degrees. But no one is wholly free of them. To suppose that would be to suppose that he or she had no sense at all of any way in which things ought to be other than as they are. And there is no one like that. No one thinks that the world is perfect, for only a person with no desires could think that – but that is to be dead.

Chance

One way to express much of what I have been saying is that our lives very largely escape our control and are a matter of chance, not choice. No one chooses to be born, or when and where to be born, or who his or her parents are, or what mother tongue he or she speaks. No one chooses his or her basic psychological proclivities and tendencies, or early formative experiences. Psychological patterns are largely laid down by the time one is old enough to start thinking about them, and seeking to channel or change them. Moreover, much of what happens to us as we pass through life is chance – it is chance, for example, that we meet particular people, or are subject to specific illnesses or difficulties. And because so much of what we are and what we experience is a matter of chance, we face the world as very weak creatures, exposed in all kinds of ways that can hurt or harm us. That is another way of expressing the point that we are physically, psychologically and ontologically fragile creatures. Indeed, it is probably in various forms of lack of control over our lives that we most acutely sense that fragility.

Adversity

The German philosopher Martin Heidegger expressed some such thought by saying that we are *thrown* into the world – and can never gain a wholly secure foothold. Put more prosaically, our reflections show us that adversity in human life is inevitable and can never be wholly escaped. This does not mean that we cannot devise strategies to reduce it or manage it better. But it does mean that one of the first things you need to do if you want to achieve this is to accept that your life will never be wholly free of adversity. In other words, you have to be realistic. This is not a counsel of despair. Quite the contrary. Being realistic about things is the first step towards changing them, and, even though things can never be wholly as we want them to be, we can certainly improve them.

This Book

That is what this book is about. I have explored four areas of life where we often experience adversity, aiming to show how adversity in these aspects of our existence can be dealt with more constructively. The areas I have taken are:

- *The family.* I have concentrated here mainly on how things look from the point of view of the child towards parents.
- *Love.* Here I have concentrated, amongst the many different forms of love, on romantic love, or eros.
- *Illness.* My approach here has been mainly to look at physical, rather than mental, illness.
- *Death.* In this chapter I have sought to explore both our fear of dying and our fear of death.

It will be immediately apparent that I could have chosen different approaches. For example, I might have explored the view parents have of their children, or sibling relations and rivalry. Again, there are aspects of death that I have left aside and not discussed, such as how to cope with the death of a loved one. And so on. But the aim has been to offer one central approach in each case, in the hope that enough detail can be given to provide some real, concrete reflection. Throughout I have drawn on philosophers and other thinkers to explore the topics in question. I have done so for many reasons, but principally because I believe that we can best make sense of our own struggles with adversity by seeing how others have done so in their lives. This is no substitute, of course, for our own reflection and our own attempts to clarify things, but it helps enormously.

So what I offer here are some suggestions about some aspects of the topics I broach. I aim to open up space for *productive thinking* on your part. Nothing I say is definitive, and you should test my advice against your own experience, feelings and thinking. But my hope is that even if you reject some given suggestion I make, by articulating your reasons for disagreeing, you will be able to make better sense of the adversity in your life, thinking more constructively about it, and experiencing that adversity more insightfully.

No book can hope to have everyone as its intended audience – a point that Nietzsche made ironically when he subtitled *Thus Spoke Zarathustra* 'a book for everyone and no one'. In the case of this book, my readership is suggested partly by the topics with which it deals, but also by the individuals – the philosophers and other thinkers – whose cases I discuss. These range from classical thinkers such as Seneca and Plutarch, to novelists such as Proust and Kafka, to contemporary writers such as John Updike. I do not, in general, much care whether a writer is classified as a philosopher or novelist or whatever, if what he or she has to say is worth listening to. We should get help in understanding our lives wherever we can.

I would, nonetheless, describe this as a book in *therapeutic philosophy* or *philosophy as a way of life*, because I seek in it to combine a level of reflection at a somewhat abstract level with detailed discussion of concrete cases, in the hope of providing material with which we can think more productively about our lives. This is why each chapter carries a title that points towards both the abstract and the concrete. There is an ancient and noble tradition of philosophy as therapy. This book intends to place itself in such a tradition.

In my view, philosophy is one of the ways of thinking of the human condition that can help us make better sense of it. People sometimes ask: What is the good of philosophy? What does it do? I would say that one answer is this: We all experience adversity in our lives, in different ways and to different degrees. Inevitably we start to think about what sense we can make of this adversity. 'Philosophy' is, in part, just the name for that thinking when it is continued in a certain direction and in a certain style. To that extent, it is simply an extension of ordinary ways of thinking. In this book I hope to give you a few pointers to help extend your thinking in this way. If I have done that, then this book will have achieved its aim.

1. Ambivalence; or, Adversity in the Family

Ours is an age deeply committed to the family. We imagine that Western culture is largely built on a conception of the affective family – the result of two individuals coming together because they love each other and whose love deepens and finds expression in the having of children. We tell ourselves that it is in a stable family that children have the best chance of starting out well in life, and we idealize the image of a couple who stay together through all of life's vicissitudes. One of our stock conceptions here is of the old couple on the doorstep of their home, waving goodbye to the children and grandchildren after a pleasant Sunday spent together. No politician could openly criticize the family and get away unscathed, and those politicians who are in favour of letting gay couples bring up children or wish to defend the rights of single parents nearly always support their view by saying that these are merely alternative or new forms of the family.

But the reality, as we all know, is much less tidy than the standard images suggest. The family, much as we want it to be a place of calm and security that nurtures us, is often far from that. It can often be a scene of conflict and even violence, and much that goes on in it can be dreadful and painful, leaving psychological damage for life. We all have to learn to live with this and make something of it, and in this chapter I aim to explore a little how we might do that. I investigate things mainly from the point of view of children in their relationship with their parents.

Happy and Unhappy Families

In his book *Thoughts on Happiness*, Alain (Émile-Auguste Chartier) tells us that there are two kinds of people: those who seek to silence others and those who get used to the noise others make. They each search out their own kind, and for this reason, he says, there are two kinds of family.

There are some families in which it is tacitly agreed that anything that upsets one member is forbidden to all the others. One person dislikes the smell of flowers, another, loud voices; one insists on silence in the evening, the other in the morning. This person does not want anyone to mention religion, that person finds his teeth set on edge by talk of politics. Each recognizes that they all have a right of 'veto'; all avail themselves of this right imperiously ... This makes for a dreary peace and an irritated happiness.

There are other families where the whims of each are sacred, loved, and where it never occurs to anyone that his delight could be annoying to the others ... These are egoists. (*Propos sur le bonheur*: 83–4)

We all know what Alain is talking about, and we might find a complement to what he says in Tolstoy's famous first sentence of *Anna Karenina*: 'All happy families resemble one another; each unhappy family is unhappy in its own way'. This could mean many things. One interpretation is that there is little to say about a happy family – and much to say about an unhappy one. Some confirmation of this is found in Edmund Gosse's story of his childhood and his relationship with his father. In *Father and Son* he recalls many of the difficulties of his relationship with his father, who oppressed him with an intolerant and dogmatic religious outlook, but he tells us that on one occasion he spent time with the family of his cousins and was at ease and happy. Yet, he says, he can recall little of what he actually did whilst staying with his relatives:

> This long visit to my cousins . . . must have been very delightful: I am dimly aware that it was: yet I remember but few of its incidents. My memory, so clear and vivid about earlier solitary times, now in all this society becomes blurred and vague . . . [O]f this little happy breathing-space I have nothing to report . . . [Here was] a brief interval of healthy, happy child-life, when my hard-driven soul was allowed to have, for a little while, no history. (*Father and Son*: 47)

Of course, we do often remember good times, but Gosse's point alerts us to the fact that usually we are not *puzzled* by pleasure and happiness, and hence not especially driven to reflection on them, not least because when we are happy we are simply absorbed in what we are doing and the mind meets no resistance whose nature it wishes to fathom, perhaps in order to remove it. We *accept* happiness when it is there; it does not raise problems for us. Hence, we are not really very good at distinguishing the different kinds of happy family. However, Alain is easily able to distinguish two kinds of unhappy family, and gives us the sense that part of the problem in each case is that of living in an *extreme*. He shows us that finding peace and contentment in the family – as elsewhere – is about learning to be a kind of tightrope walker, balancing acrobatically in such a way that not only does one not fall but one retains one's balance with grace.

Balancing Acts

In the first volume of Proust's *In Search of Lost Time*, Marcel, the narrator, describes a scene, a moment, one evening in his young life that has much to tell us about family life – and about why achieving that graceful balance is so difficult.

Marcel's mother is in the habit of coming to his bedroom to say goodnight and give him a kiss. On the evening in question, however, when M. Swann, a friend of Marcel's parents,

The grace and balance of the tightrope walker have much to teach us about the attitude we should adopt towards family relations.

is with the family for dinner, Marcel is sent to bed before the adults are to eat, and, just as he is about to kiss his mother, the bell for dinner rings and the opportunity escapes him. Marcel goes up to bed, wretched. He conceives a plan to send down the maid, Françoise, with a note to his mother asking her to come up to see him. He tells Françoise that his mother wanted him to send a message about some object she had asked him to look for – he does not want to admit the true reason for sending the note. Françoise probably does not believe him, but hands over the message anyway. Marcel's mother sends back word to him: 'There is no reply'. Devastated, Marcel decides to wait up in his room and waylay his mother later when she goes to bed.

Towards the end of the evening, he hears Swann leaving. Then he hears his mother ascending the stairs. He goes out from his room to meet her. She is astonished to see him – and angry. He implores her to come and say goodnight to him in his bedroom, but she simply tells him: 'Run, run, so that at least your father won't see you waiting here as if you had gone mad'. Both Marcel and his mother know that Marcel's father would be highly likely to see the boy's behaviour as feeble and self-indulgent. But it is too late: Marcel's father is already on the stairs and sees what is going on. To the surprise of both, however, Marcel's father, seeing that he is overwrought, tells his wife to go with the boy and to have a bed made up for herself in his room: she should spend the night with him. She objects, not wanting to give in to Marcel's hypersensitive nature – both his parents are aware that it is only doubtfully good for him, for his future, that Marcel be so extraordinarily acute about such things. But she has the bed made up.

'I should have been happy: I was not,' reports Marcel. He goes on:

> As it seemed to me, my mother had just made her first concession to me, which she must have found painful: for the first time she had given up on the ideal that she had devised for me, and it was the first time that she, otherwise so courageous, had had to admit defeat. It seemed to me that, if I had just been victorious, it was over her, that, if I had achieved what only illness, sorrow or age should have achieved – a loosening of her will, a bending of her judgement – then this evening was the beginning of an era, would remain as a sad date. (*À la*

recherche du temps perdu I: Du côté de chez
Swann: 38)

There are, I think, two key things that we can
learn from this. The first is that Marcel has
grasped, fully grasped for the first time, that his
mother is someone else, that she has her own
life, that the centre of her consciousness is not
his. She is the source or centre of all that is good
in his life – the missed goodnight kiss is a synecdoche for that, expresses it in compressed form.
But when she withholds herself from him, as
she does when she does not come to see him in
his bedroom, Marcel realizes that this goodness
is not in his control, that it can be withdrawn
from him in an instant. It is not just that his
mother's failure to come to see him makes him
feel wretched; it is that Marcel understands how
intensely fragile is his hold on the things in this
world that nourish him.

The second important thing in this episode
is the fact that when Marcel gets what he
wants, he is not happy. He is not happy because
when his mother comes to him she seems
changed, because he has *made* her come to
him. What he wanted was for her to come to
him of her own accord, without any constraint

on his part. In gaining his victory over her he has changed her, however subtle that change might be. A chasm thus opens up for Marcel and it separates him from his own desire. We normally think that there is nothing more characteristic of us than the desires we have: my desire to write this book, for example, is in many ways deeply expressive of the person I am – I can hardly imagine my life without my ever-recurrent desire to read, to reflect, to learn, to write – and we all have patterns of desire that seem typical of us as individuals. But Marcel is separated from his own desire: he gets what he wants and it makes him unhappy.

Someone might say, by way of objection: Marcel did not get what he wanted, because he wanted his mother to come to him unchanged. But this is to miss the point about Marcel's desire. He really did get what he wanted, but he did not really understand what it was that he wanted. Our desires are often like this: we realize, once they are satisfied, what it was that we had actually been wanting all along, because before the satisfaction of the desire we had not understood the price we would have to pay. It was not that we had not really wanted whatever we desired; it was that we had not understood the nature of our own desire.

Of course, this is not to deny that one can satisfy a desire and then realize that one did not really want whatever it was at all. But Marcel's case is of the more subtle variety already described.

Ambivalent Feelings

Marcel discovers that the experience of desire is always implicitly or potentially *traumatic*. In particular, he discovers that his desire for his mother is traumatic. Melanie Klein, the psychoanalyst, might put the point in terms of *ambivalence*: what Marcel discovers is that he can feel hostile towards that which is the source of goodness – his mother – precisely because that source can be withheld from him. He has to learn to bear the independence from him of that which is good in life, and he has to learn to bear the ambivalence of his feelings about that source. For Klein, being grown up is in large part about being able to negotiate those feelings of ambivalence engendered by the very recognition in question.

Part of Marcel's problem, of course, is that he comes to see his mother as *limited*. According to Sigmund Freud, in his short but very powerful essay 'Family Romances', and in a series of thoughts echoed in the work of Klein, this is one of the most deeply painful moments in life. The child starts out, he says, believing his parents to be 'his only authority and the source of all he believes in. However,' Freud goes on,

> as the child develops intellectually he cannot help gradually getting to know the category to which his parents belong. He gets to know other parents, compares them with his own, and so becomes entitled to doubt the incomparable and unique status once attributed to them. Small events in the child's life which induce in him a mood of dissatisfaction provide him with an occasion to start criticizing his parents, and the knowledge he now has, that other parents are in many respects to be preferred, allows him to support this attitude . . . The reason for such a reaction is obviously the feeling of being slighted. There are all too many occasions when a child is slighted, or at least feels that he has been slighted, and that he does not completely have his parents' love . . . ('Der Familienroman der Neurotiker': 227–8)

The description fits Marcel perfectly.

Even if we do not accept all the details of their respective accounts, between them Freud and Klein put their finger on an important truth: we are pretty much all like Marcel. That is, whilst there may be some exceptions, in the main we all want our mother – or, more generally, our parents, and siblings if we have them; in short, our family – to give us the kind of love and goodness that Marcel felt so agonizingly present in that withheld goodnight kiss. The inevitable failure of our parents and siblings to give us this can make the family a scene of trouble and pain, even though it can be a place of warmth and security.

And the failure is indeed inevitable, since, as George Eliot puts it, '[w]e are all of us born in moral stupidity, taking the world as an udder to feed our supreme selves' (*Middlemarch*: 243). The family is the first place where we grasp the independence of those around us. As we learn that they give us what is good but can also withdraw that goodness at any time – by choice or otherwise – we also learn that we are not the centre of the world, that the self must accept privation as central to its existence. The family, which seems to promise so much, indeed the denial of that truth, becomes the place where it is played out.

Idiots and Jesters

The truth to which these reflections point is that we never grow up. We are always potentially capable of slipping back into the mode of behaviour of the child who stamps his feet in anger and frustration because he does not get what he wants from his parents.

I was reminded of this recently when I saw a bickering couple at a railway station, on the opposite platform. Shouting at each other, they were evidently extremely angry with each other, and then she walked away from him, down the platform: 'I don't give a damn about you!' was her message. He trailed after her, yelling at her all the while. I remembered times when, as a child, I would walk away from my mother in this way, damning her and yet needing her to follow after me, and I saw in this couple the repetition of a child's reaction to his or her parent. And we have all, in various ways, been one member of that couple, walking off or standing watching as the other departs, aware of the idiocy of what we are doing and yet seemingly incapable of stopping ourselves from doing it. Perhaps that is the key point: we should never forget our own idiocy.

We should remember how absurd we are, because by doing so we might be better able to manage those moments in which we regress to the condition of children. We should try to laugh at our own idiocies – that might well diffuse those situations in which, like the couple at the station, we spoil things for ourselves and others and achieve nothing. We always secretly believe that we are the tragic hero of our own conflicts. But think of yourself as a jester instead. Then you might find that you achieve a better balance between what you want from another person and what you actually get from him or her.

Heading off Guilt

Those who are moved to write of their parents often express a deep sense of loss, of pain – of what Franz Kafka, in his unsent *Letter to my Father* (recently translated under the title *Dearest Father*), called being 'inwardly wounded'. Kafka uses the phrase in the context of an account of a moment 'from his earliest years'. He writes:

I was moaning continually in the night for water, certainly not because I was thirsty,

Thinking of yourself like this will probably help you reduce adversity in your life

but probably partly in order to irritate, partly for pleasure. After you had issued several threats, but to no avail, you took me out of bed and carried me onto the veranda and left me standing there alone for a while in my shirt in front of the closed door. I do not say that that was wrong; perhaps it was at that moment the only way to get some peace in the night. But I do mean by recalling this to describe your way of bringing me up and its effect on me. Afterwards, I was, indeed, at that time very obedient, but it left me inwardly wounded. Given my nature I could never reconcile the normality of my pointless crying for water with the extraordinary terribleness of being carried outside. Years later I still suffered from the tormenting idea that the huge man, my father, the highest authority, could, for almost any reason, come in the night and carry me from my bed onto the veranda – and that I was thus nothing to him. (*Brief an den Vater*: 10)

Kafka's father, Hermann Kafka, was a physically massive man, and he had a dominating temperament to match. The highly sensitive boy

was spiritually crushed by the bullying ways of
his father – Kafka's letter is a painful record of
incidents of the kind quoted here. Yet what is so
extraordinary is that Kafka is at pains to be just
to his father – witness his almost exaggerated
insistence that what his father did when the boy
was crying in the night was perhaps not wrong.
This is part of his general strategy in the letter
– in his life – to come to terms with his father.

Kafka describes how he believes his father
sees their relationship, and he lists the things
he himself has done or failed to do, or aspects of
his personality, that, he is sure, must have disappointed, frustrated or angered his father. He is
sure that his father sees him as cold, distant and
ungrateful. Moreover, he writes, his father thinks
of this as Kafka's fault – he is the guilty one.
Kafka continues:

> I am so convinced that this, your usual
> view of things, is correct that I also believe
> you to be wholly innocent as far as our
> estrangement is concerned. But I too am
> just as wholly innocent. If I could only get
> you to acknowledge that then – I shall
> not say a new life, since we are both too
> old for that – but a kind of peace would

be possible; not an end to your reproaches
but yet a softening of them. (*Brief an den
Vater*: 6)

Later he adds: 'I do not believe in the least that
there was guilt on your part. Your effect on me
was the effect that you inevitably had' (*Brief an
den Vater*: 8).

Above all, Kafka aims to absolve both himself
and his father of guilt. And he wishes to do this
by making his father see that what happened
between them was inevitable given the nature – the
differing nature – of their respective personalities.

Chemical Reactions

There is an idea implicit in the work of the
Jewish-Italian writer Primo Levi which helps
us see the issue more clearly, and understand
why Kafka's approach is so productive.

Levi was a chemist who was incarcerated in
Auschwitz from February 1944 until January
1945. In many ways, he owed his survival to his
having been a chemist. The most obvious way in
which this was so was that he was put to work
in the camp laboratory – the Nazis exploited his

knowledge – and this meant that he had shelter from some of the harshest work and weather conditions. But the second, more subtle, benefit for him was perhaps just as important.

Because he was a chemist, Levi was used to experimenting with elements and compounds and observing how they react with each other. In one of those leaps of the imagination which is so obvious that it is missed by virtually everyone else, Levi applied this way of thinking to his fellow prisoners and thence to the camp as a whole. He saw it as a kind of massive experiment designed to test how different individuals would react when put in the particular conditions of the camp, recognizing that it can be extremely helpful to think of individual human beings as resembling chemical elements with their own peculiar properties. Each reacts in a certain kind of way with other such elements, depending also on their respective properties.

So, just as, say, potassium reacts violently when exposed to air or to water, and therefore has to be stored under conditions which isolate it from such, we might think of human beings as inevitably reacting in specific ways, depending on their nature, when exposed to other individuals (or situations, for that matter).

Chemistry has some important things to teach us about interpersonal relations.

When Kafka says of his father that his effect on him was the effect that he inevitably had, we might see him as expressing the same perspective on human beings as that offered by Levi – that is, that they are like chemical elements. Indeed, Kafka invites us into thinking in this way, since he sees both himself and his sisters in what we might call *material* or *corporeal* terms – as a mixture of matter or stuff derived from their father, Hermann Kafka, and mother, Julie Löwy. For example, he, Franz, is 'a Löwy with a certain Kafka foundation' whilst his sister Valli has 'little Kafka material in her'. Hermann Kafka was a self-made businessman who had dragged himself out of a life of deprivation and poverty, someone who, as Hugo Bergmann, a friend of Kafka's, said, 'stood with both feet in his physical reality, in his business'. He was, as Kafka himself said, someone who valued 'strength, health, appetite, a powerful voice, eloquence, self-confidence, superiority over the world, stamina, presence of mind, knowledge of human beings' (*Brief an den Vater*: 7; 30; 71; 7). He was, in short, pretty much everything that Kafka was not, for Kafka himself was physically frail, emotionally and intellectually highly sensitive, cautious, timid, questioning and sceptical, and deeply unsure of himself. No wonder that two chemical elements of such differing natures would lead to an explosive reaction.

The immense value of looking at things this way is that it does much to cut the ground away from feelings of guilt. It makes no sense to blame a chemical for reacting as it does with another; it just does what it does. If we look at human beings in this way, we can also, perhaps, learn better to accept them for what they are, seeing the way they react as just a function of their individual nature. This is what Kafka is doing with his father. If it really was inevitable that he have a certain effect on his son, given their respective natures, it would make no sense blaming either of them for the situation, or for either of them to feel guilty.

Of course, there are circumstances in which this model does not apply. It might be useless, for example, if we are thinking about the criminal justice system, where questions of guilt and responsibility have a much more impersonal aspect than they do in intimate family relationships. But, within the intimacy of the family, I think that this way of thinking can be very helpful. After all, individuals' characters do seem largely fixed, and we have already discussed how the character a person has is largely a matter of chance – of what he or she is born with by way of natural talents, aptitudes and proclivities, as well as of the influence of external events. If, as Kafka did, one can look at those in the family by whom one feels let down – or from whom one would like so much more – as doing nothing more than acting from their nature, reacting to the world as their nature leads them to, then we might be able to feel less disappointed or want less from them, because we see them as simply being unable to give more. And that would be an improvement, perhaps a move towards more peaceful relations. Kafka sees the impossibility of changing his father, indeed the absurdity of trying to change him: he is what he is, and that is that. The best thing is simply to accept him as he is.

Of course, it is extremely difficult to accept others in this way. But it might help to reflect on how difficult it is to change *oneself*. Granted that it is hard to change oneself, the idea of changing another person becomes clear in all its absurdity. It is, of course, true that one can change oneself, at least in some ways and to some degree, but it is also true that this takes a lot of hard work and cannot be achieved instantaneously. Given that this is the case, you can see that it does not make much sense trying to change others. They may not even want to be changed! In such a case, what you need to do is to try to accept them as they are. As I say, this is very difficult to do, but it is something in your hands, whereas their changing is not, and so, to that extent, is a sensible thing to seek to do.

Getting Out of the Way

But, of course, Kafka also wanted his father to look at things as he did – to cease wanting him, Kafka, to change. And whether he was capable of that would be, from the present perspective, a matter of whether he happened to be the kind of chemical element that possessed the sort of flexibility required. He did not. What does one do in such a situation? One possibility is suggested by Dorothy Rowe in her book on depression, when she speaks about her sister. Rowe says that contact with her sister always sets her thinking about her childhood in such a way as to leave her feeling miserable because it brings back to her the fact that 'every day is a struggle against the effects of a chronic illness which was a result of childhood neglect' (*Depression: the Way Out of Your Prison*: 96). Hence, she tries to reduce the impact that her sister has on her by reducing contact with her. Rowe, borrowing a notion from Buddhist practice, sees this as a form of detachment, which she understands as a species of forgiveness – though different, of course, from the forgiveness so often (usually unrealistically) idealized as involving feelings of positive warmth for the person who has hurt us.

In my view, Rowe's approach is deeply humane and honest. If it is impossible to avoid being hurt by someone, then the best thing is simply to reduce contact with that person. It seems so obvious, but it is hard, because families tend to be very demanding of one's presence. There are all kinds of cultural, social and psychological pressures that demand of us that we get on well with our family – and the family itself can apply those pressures on us, just as we can apply them on ourselves. But if, as in the case Rowe discusses, there is someone in the family who keeps hurting us, and if we honestly think we can do nothing on either side to change that, then reducing or severing contact might well be the best option. No one could think it good; it is a matter of making the best of a bad job. But then, 'the best of a bad job is all we ever make of it', as Harcourt-Reilly, a character in one of T. S. Eliot's plays, remarks (*The Cocktail Party*: 124).

Making Something of It

Kafka did not resolve his problems with his father. His letter was never sent, and we do not know what its impact on Hermann Kafka would have been anyway. Probably incomprehension. But what is clear is that Kafka felt that he had been damaged permanently by the way he had been brought up by his father. He tells us in his letter that he sought desperately to escape from his father's influence but could not. For example, his several attempts to marry failed, and he felt that they did so because of his father: his father's effect on him caused him to sabotage the engagements himself. To marry, he says, would have meant becoming equal to his father as head of his own household. But this parity would have meant that he, Kafka, would have become a 'free, grateful, innocent, decent son' and his father 'an unvexed, nontyrannical, compassionate, satisfied father'. But, he says, for that to have happened 'everything that had happened would have to be undone, i.e., we ourselves cancelled out' (*Brief an den Vater*: 55). And that, of course, was impossible.

This sense of having been permanently damaged by one's parents is very common. In his autobiographical novel *Leavetaking*, Peter

Weiss tells us that in his family '[w]hen we spoke about life we had to be mournful and burdened. Life meant seriousness, effort, responsibility' (*Abschied von den Eltern*: 57). He tells of the effect on him when, twice in his childhood, he met a friend of his parents, Fritz W, whose attitude to life was wholly different. In his presence Weiss felt liberated, relieved, light-hearted. The two meetings with Fritz W, he says,

> the high points of my childhood, show me how differently my life, under other circumstances, could have developed, and they show me the treasure of unused joy which was in me, and still is within me, under the layers of sores. (*Abschied von den Eltern*: 50)

Or, in Italo Svevo's blackly humorous novel *Zeno's Conscience*, at the end of the chapter on his father's death, Zeno tells how his father stood up from his death bed and struck him on the cheek before dropping dead to the floor. The meaning of this gesture haunts Zeno for the rest of his life: was it merely a rebuke to him because he had tried to keep his father in bed as the doctor ordered? More likely it is a rebuke because '[w]e had so little in common that he confessed to me that, of all the people who disturbed him the most in this world, I was at the top of the list'. And: 'Many times, when I think about it, I am amazed by the strangeness of the fact that this desperation concerning myself and my future made its first appearance on the death of my father and not before' (*La coscienza di Zeno*: 28; 27). Like Kafka, like Weiss, he was wounded for life.

But there is something that Kafka, Weiss and Zeno can teach us, for they channelled their pain into something creative and thus made it more bearable than it otherwise might have been. All well and good, you might think, but not all of us can turn our pain into something creative. In one sense that is true: we cannot all be a great writer like Kafka, and that is just the way it is. Nonetheless, if you feel hurt in the way Kafka did, then you can write: you can write down your thoughts, your feelings, in the form of a diary, or as a letter – it need never be sent; that is not the point – to the person who has hurt you. It is extraordinary how helpful this is. It is not a matter of publishing anything, or even sharing the content with anyone. It is a matter of *externalizing* your thoughts and feelings, of externalizing *yourself*, a process which allows you to gain some distance on yourself and your life. There is something about putting your experiences into the form, the *pattern*, of writing that structures things and makes them better or more bearable. You might also write the response to your letter, on the part of the person who has hurt you, imagining how he or she might reply. Kafka sought hard to see how things might look from the perspective of his father, because this, too, helped to place and structure his own experience in a just perspective. You can do what Kafka did.

Communication Problems

Whatever else we say about Kafka's relationship with his father, however, it is clear that Hermann Kafka never made any serious effort to communicate with him. But what can be so painful in the family is that often the will to communicate and open up to another family member is deep and real, and yet somehow is thwarted. This was the situation in the case of Weiss, who speaks of his father's attitude to his children, whom

> he always avoided, and with whom he could never speak, but when he was away from

home he could perhaps feel tenderness for his children, and longing for them, and he always carried pictures of them with him, and he certainly looked at these worn, crumpled pictures in the evening in the hotel room when he was travelling, and he certainly believed that when he returned there would be trust, but when he came back there was always only disappointment and mutual understanding was impossible. (*Abschied von den Eltern*: 9)

Weiss articulates one of the ways in which human beings can find themselves awkward, inhibited and constrained with each other, even though there is no obvious reason why this should be so. This fact about our condition reminds us how little we understand ourselves. It is no surprise that greed, envy, anger and fear lead to the collapse of relationships; it is much more of a surprise that such collapse can be attendant on relationships where there is goodwill on both sides. This often happens in families, as Weiss reminds us, because we do usually want family relationships to work. The blood tie counts for a great deal. It is hard for many people to shake off the idea that they ought to be able to get on well with their family because they are bound to them by blood, something that is, in this context, deeply mysterious, physical and yet spiritual.

This sense of mystery is well brought out by Gabriel Josipovici in his novel *Contre-Jour*, an imaginary reconstruction of the relationship between the artist Pierre Bonnard and his wife, Marthe, through the eyes of the daughter they never had. The first part of the novel is a long monologue by the daughter, now an adult and living on her own, addressed to the mother. Speaking of a visit she paid to her parents, she says that she always had a sense that she had no place in the family, was hardly even noticed by her mother and father, who were closed in on themselves and simply did not know what they could do with her. And because she felt so excluded, she clung on even more tightly. However,

> [p]erhaps it wasn't really like that . . . Perhaps it was always only my fault. Perhaps I merely overreacted to a common complaint, to . . . a fact of life . . . I don't know. We act and then we try to interpret those acts, but the interpretations are only further acts, which themselves call out for later interpretation. (*Contre-Jour*: 42–3)

What Josipovici captures so well is the sense that we often do not know what we are doing, that our thoughts and emotions seem so deeply elusive when we reflect on them, even if, at the time we act on them, they seem so clear to us. It is as if we lived in two worlds, one on the surface, where we can explain what we are doing – visiting parents, seeking to establish a harmonious relationship, or whatever – and another, deeper world, where we do not *really* know what we are doing or why we are doing it, because we do not understand the deeper springs of thought and action which motivate us to do what we are doing. The meaning of it all escapes us – which can only make all the deeper the need we might have for connection with, for example, our parents.

Holding Onto That Which is Difficult

We can turn this mystery to our advantage. In his *Letters to a Young Poet*, R. M. Rilke says that 'things are not all so comprehensible and expressible as people usually want us to believe; most happenings are inexpressible, take place in a region where no word has ever ventured' (*Briefe an einen jungen Dichter*: 13). He uses this

as his leading thought in responding to the
questions and worries of his young correspon-
dent, Franz Kappus.

Kappus wanted advice about some of his
poems that he had sent to Rilke, but it turns out
that he was also, and perhaps primarily, seeking
advice about his life and, in particular, about his
deep feeling of loneliness. What Rilke encourages him to do is not to *fight* his feelings of
dissatisfaction:

> I would like to ask you, . . . to the extent that
> I can, to try to have patience with all the
> unresolved things in your heart, to love *the
> questions themselves* as if they were locked
> rooms and books written in a very strange
> language. Do not strive for answers which
> cannot be given to you because you would
> not be able to live them. And it really is a
> matter of living everything. *Live* your ques-
> tions now. (*Briefe an einen jungen Dichter*:
> 30–1)

Rilke sees Kappus's loneliness as being immensely
fruitful, because it gives him an opportunity to
find himself.

People have (with the help of conventions) made everything easy for themselves, have found the easiest side of that which is easy. But it is clear that we must hold onto that which is difficult. All that lives holds onto that, everything in nature grows and defends itself in its own way and is its own for itself, seeks to be itself at all cost and against all resistance. We know little, but that we must hold onto that which is difficult is a certainty that will not leave us. It is good to be lonely, for loneliness is difficult. (*Briefe an einen jungen Dichter*: 49)

Crucially, he recommends that Kappus look at things as a child does:

To go into yourself and for hours meet no one – that is what one must be able to achieve. To be lonely as one was as a child when the adults went around involved with things that seemed great and important because the grown-ups seemed so occupied and because one understood nothing of what they were doing. (*Briefe an einen jungen Dichter*: 42)

Rilke sees such a state – in which the activities of people seem odd or strange, as they do to his imagined child – as profoundly positive. For it allows a kind of *detachment*.

Love and the Spectacle of the World

We can apply this to family relationships. If we are frustrated or angry with those in our family who do not give us what we want and need, we are likely to feel lonely. We naturally seek to rid ourselves of these negative feelings by trying to get what we want. But if we allow the loneliness in question to live in us, Rilke suggests, instead of fighting to disburden ourselves of it, we realize that we are closer to finding some peace of soul. This is because the frustration and anger *attach* us all the more to the condition from which we are seeking release. In other words, accepting the loneliness that is the other side of the frustration and anger in question can lead to the dissipation of these negative emotions. What we must do, Rilke suggests, is cultivate the loneliness of the child, in which one *does not understand*. That is, we must accept the mystery of our inability to get from others what we would like; we must make the mystery of family relations something we *live*, as Rilke puts it, not something that we seek to be rid of. Hence he writes to Kappus:

> Avoid adding to the drama that is always stretched out between parents and children; it uses up too much energy and wastes the love of elders, which has an effect, and is warming, even when it does not understand. Do not ask for advice from them and assume that you will not be understood. But believe in a love that is kept for you like an inheritance and trust that in this love there is an energy and a blessing from which you do not have to escape in order to go very far! (*Briefe an einen jungen Dichter*: 35–6)

You might think that what Rilke is advising, however difficult, at least makes sense if love is there. But what if it is not? I think that, though this question is understandable, it misses the point Rilke wants to make. The love in question may not be a love that parents have for their children. When Rilke asks us to believe in a love that is like an inheritance, I think he is asking us to believe in a love that *we* can cultivate by accepting loneliness and the mystery of family relations, and *living* our questions. This is why he counsels Kappus again and again to pay attention to the things of this world – the night sky, the wind, the trees, the animals. *Here*, he says, is a source of closeness to things, of love of the things of this world.

His point is that if the world offers these things to us and is worth loving, then it is our parents who gave us the possibility of responding to the world in this way in the first place. That is their inheritance of love to us. We may never have the relationship we want with them. We may even, as Dorothy Rowe suggested, have to reduce contact with them or break it off altogether. But Rilke would say that this is a way of *living* our questions; he would remind us that we have inherited life itself, which is an inheritance of love. And, of course, to love in that way can itself lead us away from frustration and anger.

No one can say for another whether he or she might be able to find things good in the way Rilke suggests is possible. What we make of his thoughts lies in our hands, and with the expanses and limitations of our own character. But I would say: you should try to do what Rilke suggests. Try to open your eyes to the endless extraordinary sights of the natural world; we go round most of the time in a kind of routine, dazed as to what is there. But the plants, trees, animals, sky, sea, and so on are there to be seen, marvellous in their utter gratuity. If we open our eyes, we might be able to be consoled for the pain we carry within us. And if we are consoled in this way, we may be reconciled to the sense of disappointment or loss or hurt we might have concerning our parents. They, after all, gave us this life. It is thanks to them that we can marvel at the world at all.

2. Incomprehension;
   or, Adversity in Love

We are obsessed with love. Everyone is search-
ing for it or thinking about it. Or so it seems, to
judge by the number of advertisements for Internet dating websites on trains, buses and the
London underground, and by the number of such
sites themselves: there may be as many as 8,000
online dating services worldwide, and there are
even specialist web-dating sites for Christians, for
Oxbridge graduates, for herpes sufferers, for those
who especially love pet animals and for those
who want to date using mobile devices ('No-frills
Mobile Dating that's *super safe* and actually works
on *every* mobile phone, smartphones and dumb-
phones alike'; 'love is in your hands™'). There are
also sites for those with military interests or who
like wearing uniforms, for hippies, for vegetarians,
for those who consider themselves ugly ('dating
for the aesthetically average'), for fans of Star Trek
and all things science fiction, for chavs, for geeks,

goths and greens . . . the list goes on. There is also the seemingly endless supply of contemporary films and novels that celebrate romantic love; our contemporary idea that the principal motive for marriage is, or should be, love and that any other reason for marrying – say, financial security – is rather ignoble; our endless interest in the tittle-tattle that surrounds the love lives of celebrities and our suspicion that, even in their miseries, they are getting something out of love we are not and would like to have; and so on.

It is evident that we see something in romantic love – and it is romantic love I want to discuss in this chapter – that suggests to us the promise of something deeply important and almost irresistible. But we all know that that promise is often disappointed: divorce rates are rocketing, pre-nuptial agreements suggest that we know we are likely to be let down, and we are all familiar with the agonies of the loss of the one we love, or unrequited love, or just the sensation that the person we love is quite different from the person we thought he or she was. What is it that we are looking for in love? And how can we make better sense of love's disappointments and the conflicts that it so often brings with it?

Falling in Love

Since at least the time of Socrates and Plato in the fifth and fourth century BC, romantic love has been identified as a form of madness or intoxication. The deity of romantic love was Eros, and it is therefore also often referred to as eros. In the nineteenth century, Stendhal repeated the same idea, speaking in his book *Love* of 'the madness known as love, a madness which ... provides man with the greatest pleasures that are given to beings of his species to taste on earth' (*De l'amour*, 39). There is no doubt that this madness or intoxication is central to romantic love. For most of us in the modern bureaucratized world – the 'administered world' as Theodor Adorno put it – life occurs within massive organized structures that we do not fully understand and even less control – I mean, principally, the workplace. Moreover, as the sociologist Max Weber made clear, we in the modern West live in a world that is largely disenchanted: the ancient gods have left us, and the Christian God is dead for many of us, as Nietzsche famously said. Ours is a flattened world, in which mystery has been replaced by scientific explanation, and nature's meaningfulness has been ousted by the blind forces of evolutionary biology. Hence our deep attraction to the intoxication of love.

For in this intoxication we suddenly have a sense of something so much deeper and more real than our ordinary world with its tiresome duties, commitments and responsibilities, and with its prosaic flatness. The sense of abandon, of letting go, that accompanies romantic love stands in such a sharp contrast to our quotidian activities, and provides such a sense of release from them, that it is no wonder that we are seemingly irresistibly drawn to eros. Indeed, eros is really Eros: he is the only god many of us have left, and divinizes a world in which it is otherwise difficult to find meaning. Of course, this experience of eros is not new to us, as my reference to Socrates and Plato makes clear, but it has a special meaning for us in modernity.

Eros, then, is a kind of escape. But it is also a kind of escape that enables us to feel at home in the world. That was what the old religions did; they gave us a sense that this world is our home, that we can find our meaning here, even if that meaning eventually led outside the world to the kingdom of God. The experience of romantic love, precisely because it makes not simply the beloved person but *everything* lovely to behold, is an experience that seems to give us a sense of homecoming, of finally being at peace with the world.

The Legacy of Christianity

Many of our thoughts about love come from Christianity. Crucial are the ideas that love is utterly unconditional, eternal and wholly unselfish, as Paul tells us in 1 Corinthians 13: 5–7: 'Charity [i.e., love] . . . seeketh not her own . . . beareth all things . . . never faileth'. Paul was talking about a kind of love other than the romantic variety, but we often fantasize that his sentiments apply to eros. We suppose that in romantic love we fully see the reality of the beloved and are wholly concerned about his or her welfare – in other words, we are generous, kind, tolerant and patient.

What this means is that we are able to combine the intense intoxication of romantic love with a belief that what we are experiencing is wholly admirable, since it is perfectly selfless. It seems too good to be true: in romantic love we feel ourselves to be inebriated, our lives to be irradiated with meaning, the world to be filled with loveliness *and* that we are wholly selfless.

Crystallization

It *is* too good to be true. And if you want to avoid some of the disappointments of love, you should be as coolly realistic about what eros is as it is possible to be.

In *Love*, Stendhal sought to understand, and at the same time overcome, his unrequited love for Mathilde Dembowski. He had met and fallen in love with her in 1818, but she never returned his love, and the more insistent he became, the further she retreated from him. In his book, he formulated one of the most acute insights into the nature of romantic love. He called it the process of *crystallization*. If you love a woman, Stendhal writes,

> you take pleasure in endowing her with a thousand perfections ... In the end you overrate her as utterly magnificent, as something fallen from Heaven, whom you do not know but is sure to be yours.
>
> If you leave a lover with his thoughts for twenty-four hours, this is what you will find:
>
> At the salt mines of Salzburg, they throw a small leafless wintry branch into

the depths of the abandoned excavation. Two or three months later they pull it out covered with a shining deposit of crystals. The smallest twigs, no bigger than the claw of a titmouse, are studded with an infinity of dazzling and shimmering diamonds. The original branch can no longer be recognized.

What I call crystallization is a process of the mind which draws from everything that occurs new proofs that the loved one is perfect. (*De l'amour*: 34–5)

Stendhal thinks, furthermore, that what he calls a second crystallization occurs, in which the process of attributing perfections to the beloved is *deepened* by any doubts the lover may have about whether he is loved in return. In order to allay his doubts, he searches for evidence that she loves him and, when he finds this evidence, 'crystallization begins to reveal new charms' in the beloved. And although the whole process of crystallization may have started with a sense of the beauty of the loved one, the 'lover will soon come to find his mistress beautiful just as she is, without thinking about her *real beauty*.' (*De l'amour*: 36; 52)

Often we are attracted to others, not so much on account of what they are, but because the things they own or have make them seem extraordinarily appealing.

Obviously enough, Stendhal is articulating the importance of *imagination* in the whole process of love. Crystallization is only one example of this. Other examples include the role the imagination plays in making another person appeal to us not because of any intrinsic qualities he or she possesses, but rather on account of, say, the context in which we meet this person, or some other attribute, such as fame, for instance. It is well-known, for example, that perfectly average-looking people can seem wildly appealing, even beautiful, on account of the material goods they own or their profession. In such cases, the imagination is excited by the trappings surrounding a person, rather than anything about what he or she is really like, and, so to speak, the imagination mistakes the person, investing him or her with the glow of these trappings. Indeed it is extremely likely that there would be no such thing as romantic love without a large contribution from the imagination, which invests in the beloved a tangled mass of hopes, longings, desires, needs and fears which may have little to do with the person in question. And the difficulty is not so much that the imagination plays a role in romantic love as that it can blind one to what is going on. Stendhal comments:

> From the moment he is in love, the wisest
> man no longer sees anything *as it really
> is*. He underrates his own qualities, and
> overrates the least favours granted by his
> beloved. Hopes and fears at once become
> *romantic* and *wayward*. (*De l'amour*: 55)

The word 'wayward' is in English in Stendhal's
original French text, which heightens the strangeness of his description of what is happening to the
lover. In any case, there is a lesson in all this for
those disappointed in love, or for those who have
to suffer unrequited love. Stendhal is offering a
kind of therapy applied to romantic love. The aim
is not to stop us ever feeling it – it would be absurd
to embark on such a project anyway – but to
enable us to cope better with its disappointments.
He says: if your love for another is unrequited or
is full of pain, then remember that, especially
in its early stages, it is a kind of madness, something that at least partially blinds you both to the
nature of your beloved and to your own condition.
If you can do this, you might, with luck, be able
to gain a certain kind of distance from it.

Another way of coping with disappointment in
love is to make the pain part of your deeper understanding of life. I have a friend who went through

a period in which he had more than his fair share of unsuccessful love affairs. He often felt wretched and miserable. But gradually I understood that there was something willed by him in his various liaisons, because he knew that by embarking upon them he was feeding his curiosity about the human scene. There was a way in which he wanted to affirm all things, good and bad, and these relationships were one route to that. Jean-Paul Sartre was like this too. He wrote in his war diaries:

> It seems to me that, at this moment, I am grasping myself in my most essential structure: in this kind of desolate greed to see myself feel and suffer . . . in order to know all 'natures' – suffering, pleasure, being-in-the-world. It is precisely *me*, this continuous, introspective reduplication; this avid haste to put myself to good use; this scrutiny. I know it – and often I'm weary of it. That's the source of the magical attraction dark, drowning women have for me. (*The War Diaries: November 1939–March 1940*: 62)

There is something deeply admirable about such a stance. For sure, you have to be pretty stoical to see things this way, and you will run the risk of destruction if you live like this, but if you can see unrequited love or disappointment in love as a window onto the varieties of human experience, and to that extent as something to be welcomed, you will certainly learn something valuable about yourself and about life, and that itself will help make sense of the pain.

Getting Real

Stendhal is not, in any case, a cynic, despite his talk of madness. He is not denying that romantic love is valuable or claiming that such love does not really exist. As we have seen, he thinks that it is our greatest pleasure. But he *is* being realistic, and he does think that we can help ourselves by ridding ourselves of some of the illusions we have about love, amongst them those we have recovered from Christianity.

Choices, Choices

One of the central illusions from which we suffer in love is to suppose that we choose our beloved.

We often contrast this with family relationships: you cannot choose your family, we think, but you can choose your friends and those you love. It is partly because we think this that we can often suffer from very unproductive guilt when things go wrong in a romantic relationship. 'If I have chosen to be with this person,' so the thought goes, 'I really ought to be able to make it work, and if I cannot, if we cannot, then it is right to feel guilt and shame.' In one way or another, implicitly or explicitly, such thoughts often haunt those who have to live with the consequences of a failed romantic relationship.

But I think that it is largely an illusion that we choose those whom we love. Apart from the fact that it is more or less completely a matter of chance whom one meets anyway, the truth is that the reasons we are attracted to someone else in the first place are deeply mysterious. We are much less in control here than we like to suppose. A person of kindness and virtue, in whom we find nothing to which to object, can leave us indifferent or cold from a romantic point of view, whereas someone else who is without these virtues may, for reasons that are almost completely unclear, appeal to us profoundly. Perhaps, as Stendhal says, it is his hat that is the problem:

A generous man showers a girl who is unhappy with the most delicate kindnesses; he has every virtue and it seems that love will be born. But he wears a shabby hat, and she notices that he mounts his horse in an inelegant manner. She tells herself with a sigh that she can never respond to the attention he gives her. (*De l'amour*: 51)

The mystery is how a mere hat can make all the difference. But it can, perhaps because in some enigmatic way it symbolizes something for the potential lover that she finds unpleasant. Or, of course, someone's hat might work in the opposite way and attract us on account of the symbolic charge it carries for us. But the effect a person's hat has on us, in one way or another, is not something we choose.

It is very important to remember that what makes us fall in love with someone might be some minor aspect of his or her manner, or way of moving, or style of speech. It is important, because believing that we have control over our love, over our loves, can lead to those forms of self-reproach that I mentioned earlier. This is not to say that one should not work at love: beyond the first period of intoxication, and when a measure of sobriety returns, one will certainly need to do that. But it *is* to say that love is not, contrary to received wisdom, unconditional. If you are in a relationship with someone and things begin to go wrong, then, unless you have had enough of the whole thing, you will want to find solutions to the problems. But it is important that you do not make things worse by insisting that true love is unconditional and berating yourself for your incapacity to love in such a way. It is better to be honest and seek to find and nurture those contingencies which sparked the love in the first place. Of course you will need to talk things through with your lover, but you might also be able to help your relationship even more by buying your partner a quirky hat – or going to see a madcap film together, or inviting friends out for a meal with you both: this would be part of what Nietzsche calls being 'superficial out of profundity'.

What we need so often is to see the other as we first saw him or her, and this is one reason why Alain, in his short essay on the life of the couple in his *Thoughts on Happiness*, proposes that one solution to such problems in life might well be to spend time, as a couple, with others. Being with others means that we must be polite, he suggests, and this itself works positively to dissipate negative emotions. Moreover, the company of others occupies the mind and distracts from a destructive self-indulgence. 'This is why', he adds, 'one must always be fearful for a couple that is too isolated and depends only on love' (*Propos sur le bonheur*: 92–3). Clearly, what Alain has in mind is that, in company, you see your partner more as you did when you first got to know him or her, and this can remind you of what you liked so much about that person in the first place. If love is conditional, then nurture the conditions; do not seek to cultivate a love that can dispense with them.

Foolishness

'When we are born, we cry that we are come / To this great stage of fools' says King Lear. But we all naturally think that the others are the fools and we are not. This is why a trap that it is easy to fall into, even when your relationship is basically good, is complacency.

One magnificent exploration of such complacency is Ingmar Bergman's film *Scenes from a Marriage*. Johan and Marianne have what seems to be a perfect marriage: two beautiful children, successful careers, money – the lot. But the seeds of destruction are clear from the first scene, in which Johan boasts of his intelligence and sensitivity, and a later scene in which they clearly take themselves to be hard-nosed realists when it comes to themselves, their life, and their marriage. They obviously think themselves above their friends Peter and Eva, who quarrel violently over dinner when they visit. But it is this very complacency that destroys them. They gradually realize that they are no better than anyone else; they are just as weak, vulnerable and unsure about their lives as others. They are, in a word, just as foolish – Bergman calls them 'emotionally illiterate'. It is good fortune rather than any great talent or intelligence on their part that has kept them together. This is not to say that you do not need to work to make a relationship thrive or that talent and intelligence cannot help in this regard. But it is to say that a more helpful attitude is one of *gratitude*: to be grateful is to acknowledge the large residue of mystery in whatever it is that makes love endure. And Johan and Marianne do not see this. They think they have what they have by right. To think that is to run the risk of the kind of complacency that destroys them.

So one of the things necessary to keep love thriving is a healthy sense of one's own foolishness, as I mentioned in the previous chapter. This is not a matter of self-criticism or the desire to reduce oneself in one's own eyes. It is rather a matter of cultivating the capacity to laugh at oneself. It is a willingness to acknowledge that one knows much less than one thinks one does about what is good for one's beloved. It is a matter of acknowledging how little one understands anyone else – especially, perhaps, the person one loves – and resisting the impulse to criticize what that person thinks or feels. 'All of us are inconsiderate and imprudent, all unreliable, dissatisfied, ambitious . . . corrupt,' as the Roman philosopher Seneca reminds us pithily. 'Therefore, whatever fault he censures in another man, every man will find it residing in his own heart' ('On Anger': 40).

Friendship

It is, in short, a matter of being a good friend.

Aristotle distinguished three bases for friendship: utility, pleasure and shared virtue or goodness. Some friendships, he said, are a matter of the friends being useful to each other, as in the friendship between colleagues, or between the client and the provider of a service – say, between you and the architect you employ to renovate your house. The second type of friendship is based on shared pleasure, as in those, for example, who enjoy sports together. The final type of friendship is, says Aristotle, the best: it is the 'complete friendship . . . of good people similar in virtue' (*Nicomachean Ethics*: 1156b, 6). And it is the best, he says, because, unlike the other two forms of friendship, which dissolve if the utility or pleasure no longer exists, it is enduring. Moreover, its great value is evident in that each friend cares about the other for the other's sake, and not simply on account of what he or she can provide by way of utility or pleasure. This third type of friendship is also itself useful and contains pleasure, so it is a kind of synthesis of all that is good in the other two forms.

It is not hard to see what Aristotle is getting at, but it seems to me that he presents an overly moralized view of friendship. This is because he imagines that true friendship involves the friends in what one might call a shared project for the good, and central to their concern for each other is concern for their respective virtue, for the cultivation of virtue in each other. We can see this in Aristotle's famous claim that 'the friend is another himself' (*Nicomachean Ethics*: 1166a, 31–32) and in his idea that 'each [friend] moulds the other in what they approve of' (*Nicomachean Ethics*: 1172a, 13–14). And that seems to me not only false to the nature of some genuine friendships but also unduly normative; that is, it tells us not what friendship is but what it ought to be.

An example to make my point is to be found in the film Werner Herzog made about his friendship with Klaus Kinski, which he ironically entitled *Mein liebster Feind – My Best Fiend*, as it came out in English, but more literally and correctly 'My Dearest Enemy' (there is a play in the German on *Feind*, 'enemy', and *Freund*, 'friend'). Despite all the – sometimes massive – conflict and hostility between the two men, they were clearly very close friends. Of course, you can always insist that unless a friendship is of the kind Aristotle values, it is not a real friendship. But that is surely a case of fitting reality to the theory rather than allowing reflection to be properly responsive to the nature of reality. In truth, we love our friends in part for their faults, as Herzog loved Kinski, and, if we did not, we would have no friends, for we all have faults. Moreover, whilst friends may share certain traits

with one another, friendship involves a capacity
to be continuously aware of and accept the other
as different from us. The philosopher Richard
Wollheim is, I think, closer to the truth than
Aristotle when he says that

> [t]he essence of friendship lies, I suggest,
> in the exercise of a capacity to perceive, a
> willingness to respect, and a desire to under-
> stand, the differences between persons.
> Friendship lies in a response to the singu-
> larity of persons, and a person's friendship
> extends only as far as such singularity
> engages him. (*The Thread of Life*: 275–6)

If you want to be a good friend to the one you
love, and if you want to solve the kinds of problems that inevitably arise between lovers, then,
in all likelihood, part of what you need to do is
to take Wollheim's view of friendship to heart.

It is hard to do this, because one of the hardest
things to do in life is *to leave others alone*. We
have a natural tendency to think we know what
is best for others and to want to tell them what
to do. Reminding oneself of one's foolishness is
a way to counteract this. Moreover, I have come
to believe that pretty much all criticism is at best

pointless, at worst counterproductive, even when it is justified, certainly in the context of personal relationships. Even in those rare instances where criticism might be productive, it is a matter of extraordinarily delicate judgement, and most of us, most of the time, are likely to get it wrong. We should learn to be more cautious and circumspect when it comes to giving advice to those we love than we normally are.

Egoism

I mentioned above that one of the views about love that we have inherited from Christianity is that it is wholly selfless. We believe this in part because we tend to think of the vices as being wholly opposed to the virtues. But this is a myth. The virtues are nourished by the vices. As La Rochefoucauld puts it in his *Maxims*: 'The vices enter into the composition of the virtues as poison enters into the composition of medicines. Prudence assembles and tempers them, and uses them against the ills of life' (*Maximes*, no. 182). Vanity and self-love enter into all kinds of virtues, helping to make them what they are. Of course, as La Rochefoucauld insists, they have to be tempered, but this is not the same thing as extirpating them. And romantic love certainly has its own share of egoism. The reason for this is that such love expresses a *need* of the other. In an acute discussion of Shakespeare's *Antony and Cleopatra*, Allan Bloom brings this out magnificently. Speaking of the love the eponymous couple share, he writes:

This is not the confident and giving love so much admired in modernity. It is utterly selfish, and perhaps reveals more accurately the true nature of love as desperate need of each other. To my mind, Cleopatra's complaint to the dying Antony, 'Hast thou no care of me?' (IV.xv.60), is a more powerful statement of love than are selfless expressions of sorrow or regret. Each is directed to the other by ineluctable need. Their admiration for each other means that they must possess each other no matter what the consequences. It is a hunger and a possessiveness more powerful than any other. Few men or women are capable of such selfish self-forgetting. (*Love and Friendship*: 305)

Antony and Cleopatra may be extreme, but they only bring out something that is implicit in all romantic love, namely, its egoistic self-concern. The point is not, of course, that one should seek to be selfish in love, or that we can never see selfishness as destructive of eros. It is rather a question of being honest about its nature. As with the idea that love is unconditional, the thought that love is wholly selfless can lead to self-reproach and frustration, especially if you are confronting problems in a relationship. All relationships involve an ever-shifting balance of power, and those who hope to find stability by seeking to allow themselves to be absorbed selflessly into their lovers' needs usually find in the end that they have been complicit in something destructive. What is required is a balancing act between difference forces, not a doomed attempt to rid the relationship, or one side of it, of all force.

A Fable

The German philosopher Arthur Schopenhauer recounts a fable in which he compares human beings to porcupines. On a cold day, the porcupines huddled together for warmth, but, in doing

Human beings' quills are more difficult to see, but can inflict much pain.

so, hurt each other with their spines. So they moved apart, but in this way became cold again. Human beings, says Schopenhauer, are like this: we crave the warm intimacy of closeness with others, especially in romantic love, but, once we get it, we can end up hurting each other through that very closeness. That can engender many conflicting emotions, perhaps the most common of which, and the most likely therefore to damage a relationship, are anger and jealousy.

Anger

The ancient philosophers were especially interested in anger and how to avoid it or control it. They have some very helpful things to say. For example, in an essay on anger, which repeats some of the advice offered earlier by Seneca, Plutarch gives a large role to Fundanus, who was consul in 107 AD and, apparently, notoriously quick-tempered. Fundanus tells us how he managed to tame his anger, and recommends a number of things to us to this end. For example, he reflects on the fact that the physical aspect of the angry person is deeply undignified: distorted features, flushing face, change of voice and so on. Realizing all this, he says, he became reluctant to appear so 'unhinged' to others, and says he wishes he could have an attendant who would hold a mirror up to him whenever he is angry, in order to remind him to avoid such indignity. Then he tells us to reflect on others who resisted anger, even when anger might have been justified.

My favourite example is that of Antigonus, who overheard some of his soldiers cursing him close to his tent, unaware that he could hear them. He looked out at them and said: 'Oh dear, can't you go further away to criticize me?' Fundanus also tells us that if we are angry we should wait to act, because, once we cool down, a more moderate response may seem more sensible. Then he suggests that anger is nearly always the result of our feeling slighted or ignored, so we should seek to develop a sense of indifference to such feelings – like Diogenes who, when he was told that some people were laughing at him, replied: 'But I don't feel laughed at.' And again Fundanus recommends that we learn to be pleased with small things, to develop a simple lifestyle – not to be fussy about what we eat and drink, for example. We should learn, he says, 'not to need a lot of extras' ('On the Avoidance of Anger': 194). And Fundanus emphasizes that these strategies can help when it comes to intimate relationships.

To all this we may add Seneca's advice about seeking to know one's own limits so that one does not take on tasks that are overly demanding; failure will otherwise be likely and anger the probable consequence. In the situation of romantic love, the point is helpful: do not expect yourself to give more than you can. This is not a plea for laziness, of course, but for a realistic sense of who we are. I once asked a friend, who has been in a healthy relationship for the best part of thirty years, what the secret was. He answered: 'Low expectations'. That could be interpreted as miserably cynical, but it was not. He was being realistic – not only about what the relationship could give him, but also about what he could give to the relationship. Doing moral press-ups is much more difficult than physical ones, and usually leads to disaster. As the French essayist Montaigne put it, if you seek to fly like an angel you will crash all the more violently to earth.

Seneca also advises us to nurture the mind with 'pleasurable arts': 'pleasant pursuits prove a balm to the troubled mind' ('On Anger': 26). Applied to the context of love, this is in accord

with my earlier thought about nurturing contingencies: love is nourished through the couple's
sharing pleasure together. Pleasant pursuits prove
a balm to troubled love. The point is obvious. We
all know it. But it is worth reiterating, because we
forget it so easily.

None of this is to deny that anger can ever be
justified – though that is what Plutarch thought –
but it is an appeal to us to learn to educate our anger.

The anecdote about Antigonus is especially
revealing. For what he has clearly grasped is that
it is no use expecting *not* to be criticized. He
accepts the fact that one will inevitably be criticized, and that the best thing is not to rail against
that. His outlook is very close to something
expressed by Nietzsche in *Human, all too Human*
in the context of friendship.

> Just think about how different feelings are,
> how divided the opinions, about even the
> closest acquaintance; how even the same
> opinions in the heads of our friends have
> a quite different place or intensity than in
> yours; how hundreds of times there are
> grounds for misunderstandings, for flight
> filled with enmity. After all that, you will
> say to yourself: 'How unsure is the ground

on which all our bonds and friendships rest, how close are cold downpours and bad weather, how lonely is each person!' Whoever grasps this ... will perhaps ... cry: 'Friends, there are no friends!' But rather he will admit to himself: 'Indeed, there are friends, but error or illusions about you have brought them to you; and they must have learnt to be silent in order to remain your friend. For such human relationships rest almost always on the fact that a few things are never said, indeed, that they are never touched upon ... Are there people who would not be mortally wounded if they found out what their most intimate friends in the final analysis think of them?' (*Menschliches, Allzumenschliches: ein Buch für freie Geister*: I, 376)

Nietzsche's point is that friendship depends in part on the kind of tact that involves a willingness *not* to know all the other thinks of one, a willingness to accept that one *cannot* know these things. In other words, friendships flourish, amongst other things, *under conditions of mutual incomprehension*: your friend will inevitably remain, in many ways, a mystery to you, and that

is one of the things that nourishes the friendship. And the same goes for romantic love, as
Dorothy Rowe pointed out (*Depression: the Way
out of Your Prison*: 133–4). If you want your love to
flourish, accept that you cannot fully know your
beloved, that your beloved cannot fully know
you, and that, per impossibile, were you to know
each other fully, that would kill the love.

Jealousy

Bearing this in mind can also help when dealing
with jealousy, one of the emotions most destructive of love. Many people are subject to jealousy
in romantic relationships, and there can, of
course, be times when it is justified. However, it
is well known that jealousy, once it is triggered,
can take a hold in a way which is self-perpetu-
ating, feeding on suspicion in such a way that
there is nothing the person who is the object of
that jealousy can do to assuage it. The reason for
this is that jealousy wants something it cannot
have: it desires a kind of perfect surveillance of
another, and, even if it could achieve this with
respect to another's behaviour, it cannot do so
in the case of another's thoughts and feelings.

There are two principal reasons for this: firstly, even if the jealous person knows in a general way what the other thinks and feels, there is always room for interpreting this knowledge in order to make it seem as if it justified the jealousy in question; secondly, it just is not possible to know precisely and completely what another thinks and feels.

One of the things one should bear in mind if one is prone to jealousy is that nothing can satisfy it. Further, what the jealous person wants is, ultimately, that the other person not have a life of his or her own, as Tolstoy brings out so magnificently in exploring Anna's jealousy of Vronsky, and Proust brings out in Marcel's attitude towards Albertine. It is the thought that Vronsky and Albertine have aspects of their lives which do not involve Anna and Marcel respectively that is unbearable to them. Yet, the painful irony is, as Proust brings out, that it is precisely the sense that the other person can introduce us to a whole other world that is one of the things that makes us fall in love with him or her in the first place. That the beloved lives in a world that is not one's own and to which one can be introduced is immensely exciting, but jealousy feeds off the same sense of the otherness of the beloved. This is one of the reasons why love and jealousy so often go hand in hand: they are nurtured, in part, from the same source. If you suffer from jealousy, you should try to remind yourself not only that what you want is futile, because it cannot be achieved, but also that whatever is tormenting you is, in all likelihood, the very same thing that made you love the other person in the first place. As ever in life, one has to pay, and the idea that any condition of life could give us all we want is a mere chimera.

Beyond that, it is, of course, true that jealousy in the context of romantic love is most likely to be occasioned by sexual infidelity or fear of such. Both the experience of falling in love and the profounder love that issues from this as the relationship deepens tell us that the normal state of affairs is fidelity and that infidelity is bad. But what this way of looking at things overlooks is that fidelity is *not* something *simply* to be *expected*, but a real and deep achievement. This was expressed comically but wisely by Dustin Hoffman when he was interviewed for *Desert Island Discs* on BBC Radio 4. A friend had given him the following advice, he explained: 'the only way a marriage can be successful is that the husband is scared shitless of his wife'. Hoffman recognized that there was something profound in that because, in his view, we are – Hoffman had men in mind in particular, obviously enough – not well suited by nature to remain in a relationship with *one* person for the length of time that, these days, we often suppose the norm – as it might be, a lifetime. Commitment, he said, is difficult, requiring a great deal of diligence and discipline. Fear of one's wife, he suggested, helps keep one from straying.

Hoffman's realistic and humorous wisdom is echoed by the General's melancholy wisdom in his reflections on fidelity in Sándor Márai's novel *Embers*. Looking back on the liaison that his best friend, Konrad, had had with his, the General's, wife over forty years before, he says:

> What is fidelity, what do we expect of the woman we love? I am old, and I have thought a great deal about this too. Is the idea of fidelity not an appalling egoism and also as vain as most other human concerns? When we demand fidelity, are we wishing for the other person's happiness? And if that person cannot be happy in the subtle prison of fidelity, do we really prove our love by demanding fidelity nonetheless? ... Now, in my old age, I would not dare answer these questions as

unequivocally as I would have done forty-
one years ago . . . (*Embers*: 220)

That we find it hard to accept what is being said
here is a sign of its truth.

In Mozart's opera *Così fan tutte*, two officers,
Ferrando and Guglielmo, are engaged to two
sisters, Dorabella and Fiordiligi, respectively.
Don Alfonso (a *vecchio filosofo*: an old philosopher)
claims that, contrary to the soldiers' claims that
their fiancées will be eternally faithful, he can
prove that, like all women, they are fickle. A bet is
made. Ferrando and Guglielmo leave, ostensibly
to go to war, then reappear disguised as 'Alba-
nians'. In this guise, they manage to seduce the
two women. The truth is revealed to all, and Don
Alfonso urges the two officers to forgive their
fiancées – after all, '*così fan tutte*': 'all women are
like that' (literally, 'thus do all [women]').

Some have seen the opera as misogynistic
or cynical. But Mozart's extraordinary music,
in my view, allows the opera to transcend these
categories and show us an affirmative attitude
towards human weakness and vulnerability, an
urbane acceptance of the vicissitudes of all things
human. And we should, after all, grant that
fidelity is difficult, meaning that we could never

understand the very concept of fidelity unless we understood it as something not easily or readily embodied in human life. Human beings are fickle by nature, as Machiavelli said. Hence it is that fidelity is an extraordinary achievement, and the jealous lover might do well to reflect on his or her jealousy in the light of the difficulty of fidelity. If we start from that thought, jealousy might become more tractable, precisely because a space has been opened up to see the cause of it – infidelity – not simply as dreadful without residue, but, as in *Embers* and *Così fan tutte*, as just one more expression of the terrible weakness of human beings as they make their hesitant, halting way through life.

Of course, I recognize that such an attitude is immensely difficult, especially when one is caught up in the throes of jealousy. For this reason, it is wise to reflect on such things when calm, in *advance* of experiencing jealousy, in case one does experience it. In other words, it is sensible to prepare oneself. It is worth remembering that peace of mind does not come easily or quickly and is a rare and difficult achievement. And if we ever achieve wisdom in these matters, our hold on it remains far from wholly secure. Samuel Johnson was right, in his cautionary tale

Rasselas, to worry about fine-sounding words and have his character Imlac say: 'Be not too hasty . . . to trust, or to admire the teachers of morality: they discourse like angels, but they live like men' (*The History of Rasselas, Prince of Abissinia*: 80). But that, too, expresses a kind of melancholy wisdom, and Johnson would have been the last to take it as a recommendation that one not seek to educate one's emotional responses to the adversities of life. Indeed, his whole life stands as a moving testament to just that struggle.

The Limits of Love

In Corinthians, Paul presents love as universal in its power: it never fails, he insists. But he is wrong. It does. You can love someone you do not like; you can stop loving someone you do like; you and your partner can still love each other but be unable to be together. Love is just *one* aspect of a relationship, and by itself it is not enough to make a success of things. But part of the problem lies in what one counts as success and failure. We see the end of a relationship as a failure, but this is not necessarily the best way to think of things. Of course, no one can deny that when things come to an end, however they do, it is usually extremely painful for one of the partners or both. But I am not convinced that things are as clear-cut as we often suppose them to be.

A friend of mine told me that, though he was divorced, he did not really have the sense that he had 'married the wrong woman', as the clichéd phrase has it. In part, this was because he had had children with this woman, and nothing was more important to him than they were. Beyond that, he was puzzled by the idea that he could think of his ex-wife as 'the wrong woman', because it seemed to presuppose that there might have been, or might be, the 'right woman' somewhere: a woman with whom he would experience no difficulties whatsoever. But, he said to me, this is not so: his current relationship might be better than his marriage was, but this does not show that he 'had got it wrong' before, except in the obvious sense that the marriage ended. With his ex-wife he had had good and bad times, highs and lows – but all of that, he said, was his *life*. And though he might regret certain aspects of his life, he could not regret the whole thing.

My friend's sense of the end of his marriage expressed, I think, a kind of fierce attachment to his own life as something uniquely valuable, not despite, but because of all its errors. There is wisdom in such a view and, if you are going through the loss of a loved one, you might find that reflecting on it helps a little: if not now, then at some later point, with luck and hard work, you might be able to see things in this way. Your life is, like my friend's, uniquely valuable, not despite its disappointments but because of them, including those suffered in love.

3. Vulnerability; or, Adversity in the Body

I am sometimes struck, when teaching my students, by our good fortune. Here we are, able to spend two hours thinking about some problem in philosophy – say, the nature and meaning of religious faith, or the relationship between comedy and tragedy, or what we understand by the concept of a human being. One of the major reasons we can do this is because we are in good health – we are not troubled by our bodies in such a way as to make prolonged reflection and discussion difficult or even impossible. Of course, there are sometimes students who are suffering from some illness, more or less serious, and they are admirable in their determination to continue to study. But they represent the exception. And the fact remains that, for most of the history of humanity, most people were not generally in a state of health good enough to leave their minds free to reflect on the kinds of things that occupy my students and me in our lessons. On the contrary, ill health and sickness dogged people's lives in a way that, fortunately, is much less common in the developed world – though there are, of course, plenty of people elsewhere in the world who are not so lucky.

Nonetheless, illness has not been wholly eradicated from the human world, and it never will be. And in illness we realize how fragile and vulnerable the body is, how much we accept good health as if it were the norm when, in fact, it is more a matter of good fortune than anything we have by right. In illness, we have to face our essential weakness: the adversity of the body. In this chapter, I propose to reflect on some ways in which we might do that.

Montaigne and the Vulnerability of the Body

Towards the end of his life, Montaigne suffered from kidney stones, to which he had inherited a propensity from his father. Kidney stones are caused by a buildup of calcium or other minerals in the body, creating spiked or jagged crystals, like fragments of shattered glass. They can cause extraordinarily acute pain, not only in the abdomen but also in the ureter as they pass into the bladder; the sensation is like being burnt on the inside. These days they can be treated, but in Montaigne's day all one could hope to do was pass them out in the urine, itself an intensely painful experience. Indeed, in Montaigne's time kidney stones carried a risk of death through infection, and it is said that the pain was by itself intense enough to lead some sufferers to contemplate suicide.

In his *Essays* Montaigne speaks from time to time about his kidney stones, and some of the most revealing and moving passages are to be found in the very last essay, 'On Experience', in which he traces out some of the ways in which he sought to cope with the illness. But the essay is more than that: it is also a plea for the body, for its needs and its legitimacy, an entreaty that we accept it, together with the strange demands it makes upon us. There is in all of Montaigne's writings a calm acceptance of the body, a sense of its loveliness, even as it is vulnerable to illness. He wants us to see that, whilst our physical vulnerability makes us liable to illness, it also opens us up to physical pleasure and delight. Hence, he speaks in generous terms of our need to eat, drink and sleep, encouraging us to enjoy these things for, after all, we have no choice but to follow their demands, and he even tells us that he likes scratching himself, particularly his ear, he says, which often gets itchy.

Montaigne believed that sixteenth-century France was too suspicious of pleasure, and I doubt that he would have thought the modern world any different: what we so readily take for pleasure he would have seen as the miserable pursuit of empty satisfaction, the expression of an unavowed wretchedness which makes our pursuit of pleasure desperate even as it makes it unobtainable. He would say that our very insistence on pleasure in the modern age is a sign that something is wrong, that what we want is not so much pleasure as self-forgetfulness – the abandonment of all thought and judgement in a miserable carnival of intoxication. The synecdoche of this is the contemporary attitude towards erotic desire, in which sex is less about pleasure and more about a kind of desperate longing to escape ourselves in an abandonment to, and of, the senses so intense that it puts an end to all future pleasure, as if we could disburden ourselves of the demands of the body at one fell swoop and be liberated forever from its demands. Our hubris prevents our getting what we truly want, in part because it stops us asking what it *is* we truly want. Our age is, in its own way, as far away as was Montaigne's from accepting his advice neither to flee from pleasures nor to chase after them.

Given Montaigne's generous understanding of the body, it is not surprising that he has some things to say about being ill on which it is worth meditating. His final essay is a kind of therapy of illness. So, for example, he tells us that in confronting his own illness – not just kidney stones, though he was certainly thinking about them too – he sought neither to fight it relentlessly nor to give in to it weakly, but to allow it its place, according to its nature and his own. We must, he says, 'submit gently to the laws of our condition. We exist in order to get old and weak, to fall ill, despite what medicine offers' (*'De l'experience'*: 299). He counsels us that we should not complain if something happens to us that could happen to anyone, and reminds us that, whilst we can often look on the illness and pain of others with equanimity, we complain bitterly when we experience the same things. There is in Montaigne a kind of solidarity with others which encourages us to recognize that we are nothing special as individuals – that what happens to others can happen to us, and that that is just the way things are.

In addition to all this, Montaigne explicitly lists the things that have helped him cope with the illness caused by his kidney stones: he recognizes it as simply part of growing old; he sees that many of the men he most respects have the same disease, and he is honoured by being in their company; he is grateful that illness has come to him late in life, since he was free to enjoy his youth; and he takes delight in being praised by others for his fortitude in the face of his illness. He also points out that, in the past, some people called down upon themselves various illnesses as part of the practice of asceticism, in the belief that to do so promoted virtue. He would never do this, he says – but the illness that has come unbidden is teaching him this lesson, for which he can thus be grateful. Further, he grants that, although his kidney stones might precipitate his death, so might any number of other illnesses that he happens not to have; and lastly he says that the illness is weaning him from life, allowing him to face his own inevitable death with greater equanimity. And in an extraordinarily striking turn of phrase, he ends this part of his reflections thus: 'You are not dying because you are ill; you are dying because you are alive. Death kills you perfectly well without the aid of illness' ('*De l'experience*': 302).

In his study, Montaigne had inscribed on the beams quotations from some of his favorite classical authors. He wanted to be forever reminded of the wisdom they offered in the face of adversity.

There is in Montaigne's reflections a massive sense of reality, a capacity to grasp experience directly and for himself that is rare. He is able to see clearly what is happening to him and at the same time find consolation in his agony, without self-deception. And he is able to turn his suffering to account, to put it to use. Moreover, he helps us see that the way one thinks of one's body is not fixed; we have a certain flexibility here, a capacity to conceptualize, to imagine and to experience the body in new ways.

Very few of us, I think, possess as clear a sense of ourselves and our reality as Montaigne did. Certainly this is true in my own case. Some little while ago I was ill. It was nothing serious – mainly I was rather run down, but I also had heart palpitations and some problems with my eyes. I had a series of tests with my GP and at the hospital, but no underlying or fundamental problem was discovered. Nonetheless, the symptoms continued to get worse – dizziness, pins and needles and so on. At about this time, I was fortunate to be able to spend a few months in Italy. The moment I arrived, my symptoms disappeared: the change of climate and lifestyle snapped me out of my routines and broke the cycle of the illness. It was immediately evident to me that what had really been making me ill was my anxiety about being ill. I had been ill to start with, but somehow an anxiety about being ill had got hold of me, and I continued to be ill simply from the thought that I was ill. But I am sure that, had I been able to learn from Montaigne, my symptoms would have disappeared long before I went to Italy. This experience was all the more striking in that I am not given to hypochondria in general. I know that what I experienced is quite common: we all – most of us, anyway – can make an illness worse by not seeing it as merely part of the flow of life, by reaching out too quickly to rid ourselves of it, by fretting about it. This is not to say we should not seek medical help if we need it. But it is to say that we ought, like Montaigne, to try to be realistic about the vulnerability of our body. Ironically, accepting your weakness can make you strong.

A Narrative of Illness: the Possibility of Gratitude

Some of the points I made about how we think of the body are well articulated – though not in the context of Montaigne, whom he does not mention – by Arthur W. Frank in his helpful book *The Wounded Storyteller*. Frank explores some of the ways in which we can give a *narrative* of illness – that is, think about it, give an account of it, tell a story about it. And, in Frank's terms, Montaigne construes the narrative of his illness as a quest. Such quest narratives, he says, 'meet suffering head on; they accept illness and seek to *use* it' (*The Wounded Storyteller*: 115).

John Updike, who had a lifelong battle with extreme psoriasis, also exemplifies this kind of narrative. Having sought relief from his illness for many years by massive exposure to the sun in summer, he was eventually able to find help in a new form of treatment in the 1970s known as PUVA, a kind of UVA light therapy. And yet, once 'clear', he wondered whether there was not, after all, an intimate connection between his skin condition and his abilities and resilience as a writer. 'Only psoriasis,' he writes, 'could have taken a very average little boy ... and made him into a ... writer. What was my creativity ... but a parody of my skin's embarrassing overproduction? Was not my thick literary skin ... a superior version of my poor vulnerable own ... ?' ('At War with My Skin': 75).

Updike expresses here the capacity to *turn illness to account* – though it is only in retrospect that he sees himself as having done this. Moreover, he displays a very under-acknowledged ability to show gratitude for illness, an ability to remind himself that it is possible to be grateful for that which hurts us, because it can make us into more than we would have been without it. No doubt Updike would have taken the treatment for his psoriasis much sooner in his life, had it been available. But what he makes us acknowledge is that a cure for illness is not always something that we have good reason to want. This is not, of course, a way of saying that illness is (or some illnesses are) good; it is, rather, a way of reminding us that we can each ask for ourselves what we truly and deeply want and need in life, and that the removal of illness (as with other adversities) might well, in some cases at least, make getting closer to that more difficult.

We should all try to do what Updike did and think about whether the things we want to rid ourselves of are not part of what makes our lives worthwhile. If you want to be in perfect health all the time, and you get what you want, it might make you complacent and self-satisfied. It might make you insensitive and uncaring to others. Or it might mean that your life lacks the kind of 'edge' which can help you see the world from an individual perspective and hence be related to things in a more productive, more intense way. Illness is not always a bad thing, and it is not always to be feared.

Further Narratives of Illness: Triumph and Silence

The two other types of illness narrative that Frank mentions are what he calls 'the restitution narrative' and 'the chaos narrative'.

The former is a kind of story in which illness is construed as a temporary hiatus or deviation in the narrative of a life, after which life returns to 'normal' – that is, to its state before the illness, a state of health. This is, as Frank points out, the dominant narrative in the modern West, encouraged by the extraordinary growth in the powers of medical science. He points out that one of the disadvantages of this kind of narrative is that it can be triumphalist, as if all illness were curable; another is that it helps us conceal from ourselves the reality of death: each illness, even a terminal one, is broken down into a series of manageable and treatable maladies, helping us to evade the truth of our mortality. He describes the death of his mother-in-law in this way:

> When my mother-in-law, Laura Foote, was dying from cancer, we all knew she was dying. At least one reason why our family never talked about her dying was that until two days before she died we remained fixed on the incremental remedies that medicine continued to offer. However clear her deterioration, there was always another treatment to offer. As long as small puzzles could be solved, fixing this or medicating that, the big issue of mortality was evaded. Each specialist carried out his task with some success, and the patient died. (*The Wounded Storyteller*: 84)

The latter narrative, the chaos narrative, is no real kind of narrative, because the person is suffering so deeply that there *is* no perspective that he or she can get on the pain in order to put it into a story. As Frank mentions, the capacity to speak about one's suffering always puts one at some distance from its source, and can help one to cope with it. The deepest forms of suffering are in this sense silent. This reminds us of something we know, but often forget, namely that much human suffering is nothing more than unmitigated pain, pointless torment. We should all, perhaps particularly those who are thinking or writing about making sense of illness and bodily fragility, seek to bear this in mind, in order not to lose sight of the real nature of our own and others' suffering.

How Do You Think of Your Body?

To accompany these narratives, Frank offers different ways in which one can experience the body. Firstly there is the *disciplined* body, in which one thinks of one's body as something one possesses and needs to regulate, as one does a machine. Then there is the *mirroring* body, which is conceived of in the light of, and is modelled on, an ideal image. Thirdly there is the *dominating* body, which exists as a force against others, through which, say, anger is expressed by venting itself on them. Then there is the *communicative* body, through which one fully accepts contingency, that is, the sense that one exists in a kind of dynamic relation with the external world and that the boundaries between body and world are unclear and fluid. This notion of the communicative body may seem strange, but the best example is Montaigne's attitude to his body – his willingness to see illness as part of the flow of nature through him, and his capacity to find a sense of solidarity with those who suffer, or might suffer, just what he suffers.

Of course, we all think of our bodies in all four of these ways, and often at the same time, to different degrees and depending on the context. But, as I said earlier, what Frank's conceptual scheme and Montaigne's reflections alike help us see is that we can think of our bodies in different ways. When faced with an illness one can, with luck and perseverance, meditate on it and on one's body as Montaigne did, and this might help us to see things somewhat differently and more productively.

The Need to Find Meaning in Illness

When I said that Montaigne had a massive sense of reality, I was thinking of him in the light of a point that Nietzsche makes when he says that

Berck Plage 12/V 930

Max Blecher, an ironic hero, with his mother.

it is not suffering that human beings cannot bear, but meaningless suffering. Of course, Montaigne was seeking to find meaning in his illness, but we can sense that the meaning he sought was firmly rooted in the reality of his situation. This is so, even though he was clearly stylizing himself in his illness, that is, seeking to create a perspective on his illness that would see it in noble, grand or similar terms.

One of the characters in Max Blecher's great novel of sickness, *Scarred Hearts*, echoes Montaigne's view of illness when he says that it can make of one a kind of deeply *ironic hero*. It may even be that Blecher, who suffered from tuberculosis of the spine, saw himself in this way. The novel is set in a sanatorium, and the character in question, Quintonce, is speaking with a fellow sufferer about his condition, and about the condition of all those in the institution. He claims that every hero, in order to achieve his goal, needs both energy and willpower.

Well, every invalid displays these. In the space of one year, an invalid expends exactly the same amount of energy and willpower one would need to conquer an empire ... Except only that he consumes it in pure loss. That is why invalids could be called the most negative of heroes. Each one of us is "the one who wasn't Caesar", even though he has fulfilled all the conditions necessary for being one ... To be possessed of all the component elements of a Caesar and yet to be ... an invalid. It is a surprisingly ironic form of heroism. (*Scarred Hearts*: 84)

I am sure that Montaigne would have appreciated the faintly absurd, self-deprecating but also self-valorizing notion of the ill person – in this case, an invalid – as an ironic hero. He would have taken delight in the idea's strange, indeed absurd, combination of domestic insignificance and worldly grandeur. It would have made him laugh.

Updike, whom I mentioned earlier, provides another, altogether more earnest way of finding meaning in illness, prior to his more successful treatment for psoriasis. Reflecting on the hours he spent lying in the sun on the beach, seeking relief from his condition, he writes that he always associated this with a kind of forgiveness from God, which was, for him, 'a tactile actuality as I lay ... under the ... tropical sun. And the sun's weight on my skin always meant this to me: I

was being redeemed, hauled back into mankind
. . . from deformity and shame' ('At War with My
Skin': 68).

For Updike, the meaning of his illness was irre-
ducibly religious, because he saw it in categories
that he saw as religious: shame, and redemption
through forgiveness. It was this, in part, which
enabled him to cope with it: his psoriasis was not
simply a form of physical discomfort; it was also,
and perhaps more importantly, a kind of connection with God, mediated by the physical world
– and thus a special kind of connection with that
world. He found meaning in the illness through
the meaning he found in its treatment. A great
deal of the work of coping with illness depends
on our capacity to find meaning in it, as Montaigne or Quintonce or Updike did – and there
are, of course, countless other ways of doing so.

Indeed, I suspect that we all need to stylize
ourselves in one way or another to make sense of
illness, especially long-term and serious illness
of the kind that afflicted Quintonce and Updike.
Quintonce sees himself in the light of Caesar, and
there are certainly worse ways of seeing oneself.
His approach is much more urbane than that of
Updike. In any case, stylizing ourselves when we
are ill, and thinking about how our illness might

allow us to emulate those we admire, can be productive. Reflecting on what these individuals might say to us in our illness also helps, I think. And this applies not just to illness, of course.

Whilst I have been seeking in this chapter to draw attention to people whom it might be helpful to emulate, we each have to find our own sources of help. This is why we need to try to be attentive to others around us and the story of their lives, in order to discover the interesting, the strange, the good and the lovely in them, which we so often miss in the general rush of everyday life. By doing so, not only can we understand them better, but we can also understand ourselves better too.

Making Things Worse

But if it is true that we seek meaning in illness, sometimes we can entertain extravagant and unrealistic thoughts about it. This can make matters worse. So, for example, we often link illness and morality, construing illness as a form of punishment. Father Paneloux, in Albert Camus's novel *The Plague*, represents someone who thinks this way, at least at the outset, telling his congregation that the plague has come to their town, Oran, as a punishment for their sinful ways. This kind of thing can be found again and again in human history, and it has not disappeared. As Susan Sontag reminds us in her book *Illness as Metaphor*, illnesses – her examples are tuberculosis, cancer and AIDS – have often been used as metaphors: sometimes to blame, sometimes to punish and sometimes for other purposes, such as to control. Her aim in her book is to strip illness of metaphor – 'I have this disease because I am a bad person; this illness is a punishment', and so on – in order to remove from it the meanings that make the suffering even worse.

A good and moving example of someone who found meaning in his illness (tuberculosis), but in such a way as to make things worse, was Kafka, whose pained relationship with his father I explored a little in the first chapter. In many ways Kafka was a highly tormented man: as a German-speaking Jew in Prague he felt himself to be an outsider and lived in an almost permanent sense of unease and disorientation, deeply torn as he was between his profound need to be a writer, the requirement to earn his living, and his longing to be able to settle down and have a family. Mentally troubled

by this, and with a strong tendency to lacer-
ating forms of self-enquiry and judgement, he
constantly thought of his body as inadequate to
the spiritual demands he made on himself, and
reproached himself for just this:

> It is certain that a major obstacle to my
> progress is my physical condition. Nothing
> can be accomplished with such a body . . . My
> body is too long for its weakness, it hasn't
> the least bit of fat to engender a blessed
> warmth, to preserve an inner fire, no fat on
> which the spirit could occasionally nourish
> itself beyond its daily need without damage
> to the whole. (*The Diaries of Franz Kafka
> 1910–1923*: 124–5)

When Kafka suffered his first attack of tuberculosis in 1917, he immediately sought for a
meaning to his disease, and construed it as a
metaphor for his illness of soul. 'For secretly,' he
wrote to Felice Bauer, his fiancée, 'I don't believe
this illness to be tuberculosis, but rather a sign
of my general bankruptcy'. He also construed
his tuberculosis in terms of his relationship to
his mother, from whom he thought he had inherited it, deriving from it, he wrote in the same

letter, 'the kind of immense support a child gets from clinging to its mother's skirts' (*Letters to Felice*: 655). Kafka, of course, knew he had tuberculosis, but what he meant was that, although it was an illness, it was a metaphor for what was *really* wrong with him – namely his spiritual condition. Kafka saw his tuberculosis not simply as an illness, but as a form of *self-judgement*; it *betrayed* him. Moreover, he went on to show a further level of emotional and intellectual investment in his disease, seeing it as both sign and cause of creativity – the creativity that enabled him to write as he so deeply needed to. Furthermore, he saw it as both a reason for his not getting married and as something that might have gone away had he married.

The case of Kafka is instructive because it shows the lengths to which some will go to find meaning in their illness. It goes without saying that I am not intending to criticize him. Far from it. My point is rather that we can see in Kafka someone whose torments are made even greater as a result of the particular way in which he sought for a meaning in his illness. If you had been Kafka's friend, you would almost certainly have encouraged him to be gentler on himself. That thought might help you if you have a tendency to be hard on yourself when you are ill, even if you do not go to the same lengths as Kafka in seeking to find meaning in your pain: you might be able to turn it towards yourself and be a little kinder to yourself.

Blaming Others

But often, when we are ill, it is not simply that we can be harsh on ourselves, as Kafka was on himself: we often have a very strong tendency to blame others for our condition, even as we know that they are not responsible. I do not mean, of course, that every ill person consciously holds others to blame for the illness. When one is ill it is more likely that one will experience anger – anger with the world, anger because one thinks the world unjust, anger expressed in the thought 'Why me?' And since other people are part of the world, they are likely to become the objects of one's anger as they stray into one's path, so to speak. One *takes it out* on others. There can be great pleasure in this, even if it is an unedifying spectacle. Indeed, the narrator in Tomasi di Lampedusa's novel *The Leopard* remarks at one point that 'the intense pleasure of crying "it's your fault" [is] the most powerful that the human creature is able to enjoy' (*Il Gattopardo*: 112). But the world, as such, is neither just nor unjust; it just *is*. This is part of what Montaigne was getting at when he said one should not complain about undergoing something that could happen to anyone.

Apropos of the tendency to take out one's anger on others when one is ill, Samuel Johnson remarked: '[D]isease produces much selfishness. A man in pain is looking after ease' (*The Table Talk of Dr Johnson*: 81). And it does indeed seem, as I have intimated, to be a natural reflex of the human mind to seek to discharge itself on others for its pains and sufferings. In fact, it is arguable that much that passes for moral judgement is really this unpleasant human tendency decked out in fine-sounding words. Be that as it may, Johnson, who was ill for much of his life – he once said that he had hardly known a pain-free day in his life – was exemplary in his capacity to resist the temptation to suppose that others were responsible for his illnesses. There is a huge capacity in Johnson to cut through appearances and make us face the reality of our condition. For example, he once remarked to his friend Boswell that the latter was forever complaining of being melancholy; this, he believed, showed that Boswell liked his mental suffering. No one, he said,

> talks of that which he is desirous to conceal, and every man desires to conceal that of which he is ashamed ... [M]ake it an ... obligatory law to yourself never to mention your own mental diseases; if you are never to speak of them, you will think on them but little; and if you think little of them, they will molest you rarely. When you talk of them, it is plain that you want either praise or pity; for praise there is no room, and pity will do you no good; therefore ... speak no more, think no more about them.
> (*The Table Talk of Dr Johnson*: 81)

This is Johnson at his most stoical, and there is something almost frightening in his words, especially perhaps to modern-day readers, who live in an age proud of its willingness to speak of mental sufferings. Of course, Johnson is speaking of mental suffering, but physical illness can often evoke mental suffering, so that the two become entangled. Again, none of this is to suggest that we should forego treatment for physical illness – Johnson knew as well anyone that any reasonable person prefers health to sickness. The point is rather that we are often surprisingly ready to burden others with talk of our illnesses, as Boswell burdened Johnson. Of course, we sometimes need help from friends when we are ill, and we do need to talk with them about what we are experiencing, but the political theorist and philosopher Hannah Arendt was surely right when she said that

> we can scarcely help raising the question of selflessness, or rather the question of openness to others, which in fact is the precondition for 'humanity' in every sense of that word. It seems evident that sharing joy is absolutely superior in this respect to sharing suffering. Gladness, not sadness, is talkative, and truly human dialogue differs from mere talk or even discussion in that it is entirely permeated by pleasure in the other person and what he says. It is tuned to the key of gladness, we might say. ('On Humanity in Dark Times: Thoughts About Lessing': 15)

Perhaps if we are ill, one of the things we most need is the gladness of friendship, and we need to seek to preserve our friendships in gladness, rather than a kind of sadness which involves a concentration on the fact that we are ill. So I am inclined to say: if you are ill, seek comfort from your friends, but remember that it is gladness rather than sadness which best nourishes you, your friend and your friendship. If you manage to laugh in and through your illness, that will probably help you.

The Will to Live

Someone who took this kind of thing to heart – I mean, the importance of gladness and laughter, with or without friends – is Norman Cousins. In his classic work *Anatomy of an Illness*, Cousins describes how after a trip to the Soviet Union in 1964 he fell ill from a very rare, virtually untreatable and extremely serious collagen illness. Collagen is the substance that binds cells together, and Cousins discovered that his collagen was breaking down. He was, as he put it, 'coming unstuck' (*Anatomy of an Illness*: 33). He had, he was told, a 1-in-500 chance of recovery. Reasoning that there was little the doctors could do for him, Cousins checked himself out of the hospital and into a hotel. He was well versed in medical literature, and remembered having read about the idea that negative emotions could have a negative effect on the body. He wondered whether positive emotions might have a positive effect. The question arose for him whether 'love, hope, faith, laughter, confidence, and the will to live have therapeutic value' (*Anatomy of an Illness*: 38).

Cousins tried it out. He abandoned the standard treatment given to him by his doctors, believing on good evidence that this treatment would, in fact, do him more harm than good. He devised his own interventions, such as administering to himself large amounts of vitamin C (ascorbic acid), since some medical reports indicated that certain patients suffering from collagen disease were deficient in vitamin C. But he also devised a programme to cheer himself up, to make him laugh: he got hold of comic films, such as those by the Marx Brothers, and watched them. Incredibly, his physical symptoms started to abate. Eventually he made a pretty full recovery.

Cousins grants that the vitamin C may have had purely a placebo effect. He is happy to accept this, because it supports his main point: he is convinced that 'the will to live is not a theoretical abstraction, but a physiologic reality

Laughing at duck soup rather than eating it might help you recover from illness.

with therapeutic characteristics' (*Anatomy of an Illness*: 49), so whether the vitamin C had any effect other than encouraging him to think positively was neither here nor there. As evidence of the will to live, he presents not only his own case, but those of two other people: Pablo Casals, the great cellist, and Albert Schweitzer, the theologian and medical missionary. He says that he learnt from them that 'a highly developed purpose and the will to live are among the prime raw materials of human existence. I became convinced that these materials may well represent the most potent force within human reach' (*Anatomy of an Illness*: 79).

Obviously, Cousins is in many ways an exception, not least because he was well-read on medical matters. Moreover, his aim is certainly not to dismiss the massive advances made by modern medical science or to claim that we could do without them. Nor is he claiming that diseases such as his are caused by negative emotions or cured by positive ones. What he does believe, however, is that immunity to illness can be reduced by distress and increased by good spirits. And he is surely right that we in the modern West are becoming hypersensitive to pain, leading us to take medicines in an obsessive manner. He counsels a kind of healthy scepticism, so that we can 'steer an intelligent course between promiscuous pill-popping and irresponsible disregard of genuine symptoms' (*Anatomy of an Illness*: 101). That, of course, requires wisdom on our part. But, if Cousins is right, it also requires humour, an ability to laugh, and a kind of thirst or hunger for life of the kind he saw in Casals and Schweitzer: 'creativity, the will to live, hope, faith, and love ... contribute strongly to healing and well-being. The positive emotions are life-giving experiences' (*Anatomy of an Illness*: 96). There is a lesson in that for all of us.

4. Dissolution;
   or, Adversity in Dying

When I was about seventeen years old, my father, whose marriage to my mother had ended in divorce when I was nine, and who lived apart from us in the west of England, started to suffer from various pains in his stomach. He had always eaten rather badly, and his doctor put him on a healthier, high-fibre diet, believing that his problems were temporary. He achieved some brief respite, but the problems continued to get worse. With my younger brother, I visited my father for New Year's Eve, at which point he had been ill for some months. That evening, we sat with him in the living room of his flat, overlooking the river. He told us that he was going to die. 'Well, boys, it looks as if I have something that's going to finish me off,' he said. These were his exact words, quite unforgettable in their devastating nonchalance. He had cancer. I have no idea what we said to him in reply. We were not, I think, terribly surprised, as we had been expecting bad news. He went to bed early, and we were left there, looking blankly at each other as midnight approached and we waited for the new year. My father received no remedial treatment for his illness, only palliative. He died in a hospice the following May. I remember feeling pleased for him that the spring weather was bright and warm, and that he had been able to spend some time on the balcony outside his room before he died.

My father, like all human beings, had plenty of faults, but the way he approached his death struck me, even in my callow youth, as immensely impressive, and I still admire him enormously for his calm, his stoicism and, in particular, his absence of self-pity as he faced the end of his life.

In 1784 Samuel Johnson lay dying, suffering from dropsy, now known as oedema, an abnormal accumulation of tissue fluid. He knew that he was going to die. The dropsy had spread from his chest to his feet. He asked his surgeon, William Cruikshaw, to cut into his legs to drain them. One of Johnson's biographers, Walter Jackson Bate, continues:

Cruikshaw was afraid mortification might set in, and only gently lanced the surface.

Johnson cried out: 'Deeper, deeper; I want length of life, and you are afraid of giving me pain, which I do not value.' ... Later, when no one was looking, Johnson managed to get hold of a pair of scissors in a drawer near the bed, and plunged them deeply into the calves of each leg. The only result was a large effusion of blood ... (*Samuel Johnson*: 598–9)

Like my father, Johnson displayed no self-pity. But he was far from calm and his stoicism was of a quite different kind. Two deaths, quite different, yet similarly admirable. There is no one good death, one good way to die. But this chapter looks at some of the thoughts that might help us face our own death, if not as nobly as my father and Johnson faced theirs, then at least with a modicum of dignity. This chapter, then, is about finding some consolation in and for the fact of our mortality. It is about the possibility of finding a good death.

Someone Dies

Tolstoy's short story 'The Death of Ivan Ilyich' is one of the most powerful evocations of death one could imagine. In particular, Tolstoy brings out magnificently two central features of death: firstly, the absolute terror we can face if we think about our own death; secondly, that we find it impossible actually to imagine our own death: death is always, we like to think, something that happens to *someone else*. Tolstoy brings out Ivan's thought concerning the latter quite brilliantly. Ivan, we read, had never dissented from those lessons in logic according to which we can deduce, from Julius Caesar's being a man and the fact that all men are mortal, the conclusion that Caesar is mortal. However, writes Tolstoy, this

> had always seemed to him to be true only when it applied to Caesar, certainly not to him. There was Caesar the man, and man in general, and it was fair enough for them, but he wasn't Caesar the man and he wasn't man in general ... Did Caesar have anything to do with the smell of that little striped leather ball that Vanya [Ivan] had loved so much? Was it Caesar who had kissed his mother's hand like that, and was it for Caesar that the silken folds of his mother's dress had rustled in the way they did? (*The Death of Ivan Ilyich and Other Stories*: 193)

What is so marvellous in this passage is Tolstoy's capacity to bring out the kind of fierce attachment we have to our own experience and the way in which this cannot be grasped from an outside perspective. There is clearly a sense in which, phenomenologically speaking, for each person, the only world that exists is his or her own world. Of course, I know that I share the planet with countless other human beings and that the reality of the world far outstrips my experience of it. But, for the person who dies, what ends is not simply *his* world, but *the* world. *My* world is *the* world because anything that wholly escapes my consciousness does not exist in my world and therefore is, for me, simply a blank. And when I say that things exist that outstrip my consciousness, they exist, nonetheless, as things that surpass me in this way, in my experience of them as beyond me, in my knowledge and sense of them as such. In this sense, they are not *wholly* unknown – they are *mine* as not known.

Moreover, there is a sense in which I *make* my world. My values, needs, longings, hopes, fears, desires and so on all lead me to interpret the world in specific ways. Proust suggests that each human being is a denizen of an unknown country, unique to him or her alone. In this life we are aware of this but cannot express what that world is, yet we see *this* world as we do because of our provenance from elsewhere, from that unknown country. Only artists can express their world and, thanks to them, we are able to see this world in a new light. This is why we say that certain novelists, playwrights and so on, create a world that we can enter.

I am, of course, not making a moral judgement about individual egoism. I am, rather, seeking to capture a central aspect of how we each experience the world – that is, of the phenomenology of experience. And it is, I think, when we compare our idea of our own death with our idea of someone else's that we become most acutely aware of the way in which, for each of us, everything that exists does so in our world alone. If someone else dies, however much I care about or love that person, life goes on, the world continues to exist. If I die, then there is – nothing.

Hence the philosopher Ludwig Wittgenstein remarked: 'Death is not an event in life. We do not live to experience death' (*Tractatus*: 6.4311). It is not just that there is nothing on the other side of death, but also that to try to imagine one's own death is always to imagine it from someone else's point of view. In a sense, Wittgenstein is saying that dying is like falling asleep: there is nothing that one can describe from the inside, because the experience of falling asleep is empty – unlike, say, the experience of exhaustedly stretching out in bed to sleep. That moment at which sleep comes cannot be described from the inside. It is only when we wake up that it seems to be something, but that is an illusion.

Of course, some people think that they will wake up after death. They think that after death life goes on – say, with God. I do not presuppose such a view here. And it is, I think, because the end of my world is the end of the world that death is so terrifying.

'Death is Nothing to Us'

In the ancient world, Epicurus and Lucretius picked up on the idea that the end of one's world is the end of the world to suggest that, after all, we should not fear death. For, so the thought goes, when we are living, death is not present; and when we are dead, we do not exist to experience anything. So to suppose that death is bad for us, a misfortune, is to suppose, mistakenly, that we would be around, but dead, to experience this misfortune. But this is obviously not so. Hence, it is said, there is nothing to fear in death because once it is there, we experience nothing. On this view, death is not a misfortune at all.

Not many of those who have reflected on this argument have found it convincing. It has seemed to them that the problem is that death remains a misfortune after all because the argument overlooks the deep attachment we have to our own experience of the kind that Tolstoy brings out. Even if it is true that I will not be around to experience my own death, death is still bad for me because what I want is my experience, *my state of experiencing the world*, to continue. This does not mean that life can never be burdensome, or worse. But even if life is utterly terrible, death can still be a misfortune – it is just the lesser of two evils, but still an evil.

This does not mean, of course, that there is no consolation to be found in our mortality, or that we cannot face our death with good grace or nobility.

Death and Reality

A friend of mine was recently diagnosed with breast cancer. During one conversation we had, she said something in particular that struck me powerfully. She said she felt a certain relief in the diagnosis because it brought her face-to-face with reality. What she meant was that the fact of her possible death made real what before had merely been an abstract thought for her – namely, that she is mortal. For, whilst it is true that we all know that we are mortal, we do not live in the light of that reality. It is a reality we suppress. We know it, but we do not acknowledge it. My friend was forced to acknowledge it, to grasp her reality as a vulnerable human being destined to die. That contact with the reality of her existence was, for her, a form of consolation. This is not the same as saying that she was not fearful in the face of death or that she wanted this illness, but it is to say that her contact with reality provided for her a sense that here, now, in her life, was something that she had always known was there but had concealed from herself.

A complementary way of looking at death is to be found in the reflections offered by Philip Gould, the Labour peer and strategist, who died of cancer in 2011. Gould wrote a book, *When I Die*, and made a short film with Adrian Steirn under the same title, about his experience of being diagnosed with cancer and knowing his death was imminent. What emerges from his reflections is the extremely powerful awareness that what helped him make sense of his experiences, indeed, find through them, in them, moments of joy and ecstasy, was his capacity to accept death, to face it as his reality. '[O]nly when you accept death,' he wrote, 'can you free yourself from it ... Acceptance is the key'. In the moment of acceptance, he said, 'you gain freedom ... power ... courage' (*When I Die*: 118). Moreover, it is evident that what became important for Gould was a capacity to see not just the reality of his own situation but that his impending death could reconcile him to the world. He said that he felt at one with the world and, as part of that, emphasized the continuity of life and death.

This comes out particularly in two things he said in the film. Standing in the place where his grave would be, he said that thinking about his death was not a gloomy thing at all and that 'the community of the living and the dead', with people visiting his and others' graves, was a 'wonderful idea'. Just as significant is the following comment: 'I saw my children born ... and I saw the *incredible* massive potential of that moment. And when my father died, and the air left his body, it was as powerful as the air entering the body of my daughters'. What Gould invokes is the way in which death is of a piece with life, indeed, with the *start* of life: there is an acceptance here of the endlessly turning, ceaseless cycle of all things natural, and the belief that only by accepting one's own place in this cycle can one be reconciled to death.

Why is it that this kind of acceptance enables one to be released from the fear of death? What is really going on here? The answer is, I think, this. We spend our entire existence in a state of self-protection, self-defence. Everything we are by way of instinct, need and desire, leads us to seek our own security, the further progress of the self, the defence of what we are. The novelist and philosopher Iris Murdoch spoke in this context of 'the fat relentless ego' (*The Sovereignty of Good*: 52), and she had in mind that everything we do – from organizing our days as best we can for ourselves (work, leisure, holidays, projects and so on) to organizing our lives more generally (career, marriage, children) – reflects and feeds from a kind of unthinking egoistic self-concern. This is not to say we are all selfish: after all, your welfare can enter into what I identify as what I am, and seek to protect. Regard for another is not disguised self-regard, but it is part of what one identifies as mattering to one and making one's life worth defending and securing. And what is going on in cases like that of Gould is that, in the face of imminent death, this relentless self-concern drops away, because in such a situation *there is nothing left to defend*. This means that the self can open out to the world and accept it in a way that is otherwise very rarely possible. And this is a source of joy, not least because it is an immense relief. This is why Gould said that he had had more moments of happiness and ecstasy in the last five months of his life than for many years before. Hence it is that, in a case like Gould's, a sense of the reality of the self, its mortality, and of the reality of the world – really *seeing* the world, perhaps for the first time – come together. And this interconnection of reality, world and death, this sense that such a stance is possible, is, I think, something that might help us face death with less fear and a sense that it can be something more than merely an unmitigated loss. It remains a misfortune, but we can learn from cases such as that of Gould, and that of my friend, not to see it as only that.

I think we can put the point this way. Because the concepts of reality, world and death come together as we recognize they do in the case of someone like Gould, we can see that death is actually a central concept in our making sense of both ourselves and the world. In other words, and as many philosophers have said, our mortality is central to our capacity to make sense of the reality of the world. If we were to become immortal, we would lose a key element in whatever it is that can make life meaningful. For this reason, death is not simply something that stands at the end of life, but is immanent in it. Our living involves, in this sense, the permanent presence of death. Living is dying and dying is living. This is why I have used the concept of *dissolution* for this chapter: our life is a form of dissolution – that is, the process of dying – and finds its apotheosis in the moment of death itself. We are dying all the time. For this reason, Heidegger said that we *die*, but the animals only *perish*, since they do not stand in the same relation to death as we do.

But this piece of knowledge about dissolution is something we suppress all the time because we are so fearful of death. What Gould makes us aware of is that we need to seek to live our life in the light of this knowledge if we are to make sense of both our death and our life. Usually we can only do this, if at all, towards the end. But what he encourages us to do is not to wait until then. If we can do that, we shall perhaps feel less fear of death.

Of course, this is, inevitably, something that we can do only partially, at best: the knowledge in question will wax and wane even in those who are most acutely conscious of it. Nonetheless, there are moments for some people when they are confronted by the reality of death and then they experience life as Gould did. For example, a friend of mine was told when she was twenty-three years old that she had cancer. The terror this engendered in her was accompanied by an acute sense of life in all its magnificent richness: the blue of the sky, the song of the birds and so on. She told me that she had the thought that she must retain this sense, come what may. In fact, the diagnosis was mistaken. But even now, years later, she sometimes thinks of that moment, aware that she learnt something vital then, and sorry that she cannot always see life as she did for that brief period. But if you have had a similar experience you might be able to mobilize the thoughts and feelings in question to give you a heightened sense of life precisely because you have a heightened sense of death – and vice versa.

Regrets

In a way, Gould was lucky: he died surrounded by people he loved and who loved him, and in material comfort, with doctors to advise and care for him, and in pain but not always so much pain as to make him, for example, incapable of thought or reflection. Moreover, he was in his sixties when he died, not especially young, and had led a full and active life.

But someone who discovers or believes he is going to die might be in a quite different situation: if he is young, he might be especially struck by a sense of waste, of missed opportunities, or, whether young or not, he may feel that he has made a mess of his life and be filled with painful regrets at this thought. Indeed, the latter is the case with Ivan Ilyich, who comes to see, as he lies dying, that he has lived a lie, that his life has been all wrong. At first he is filled with horror, regret and terror. But even in this case, Ivan finds consolation: his impending death has forced him to be honest with himself about his life for the first time. He finally grasps that he has lived a life wholly in the eyes of others, accepting their judgements of value and taste without ever questioning whether they were really *his* judgements about things. His

Life can hit you with all its force when you are acutely aware of your mortality.

life has been devoid of depth, of serious reflection and of insight into his own condition. He has never given any heed to that maxim of the Delphic oracle: 'Know thyself'. When he finally sees that this is so, he has the consolation that he has at least some insight into the reality of his life.

The sense of regret at the prospect of death comes over very strongly in something that Primo Levi says in his book *The Periodic Table*. After his arrest by the fascists and before his deportation to Auschwitz, he was held in a cell and interrogated. He believed that he was going to be killed at the end of the interrogations. He writes:

> In those days in which I waited for death fairly courageously I harboured a piercing desire for everything, for all conceivable human experiences, and I cursed my life up until then, which, so it seemed to me, I had exploited too little and badly, and I felt time pouring through my fingers, slipping away from my body minute by minute, like a haemorrhage which cannot be stopped. (*Il sistema periodico*: 141)

Levi was at the time only in his early twenties and was, by his own account, a rather shy and awkward

young man, somewhat naive and intimidated by
the world. But whatever his regrets might have
been, he bore the thought of his imminent death
with great courage and dignity. This is clear not so
much from what he says as the *manner* in which
he says it – the *tone*, the *style* of his writing, which
has always impressed his readers as immensely
sober and judicious. And there is a very important
point here for us if we wish to think about our own
attitude to death and how we might find something valuable or worthwhile in our mortality.
This is that here, as in many other places in life, it
really is a matter less of *what* one does than of *how*
one does it. No one else can die my death for me. It
is an event which marks one's absolute solitude or
loneliness, for, however much help one might have
by way of palliative care or the like, death is something that has to be faced alone in a very radical
sense. It is partly this that makes it so frightening.
And in this we see the extraordinary equality of all
human beings, together with the uniqueness of
each human death: we all die, but we each die
our own death. To confront one's own death, one
needs to find one's own way, one's own *style*, as
it were, and for that there can be no formulae –
though it can be helpful to see how others have
confronted their death.

Is Death the Worst that Can Befall Us?

In any case, what Levi came to realize is that there are things worse than death, and this very thought can be helpful to us in facing our own demise.

Levi was well aware that the ancient philosophers were much preoccupied with death and the fear of death. They thought that central to virtue was a kind of contempt for death, and they even conceived of the practice of philosophy as a preparation for death, since it requires a kind of contemplation disassociated from the body, which thus resembles death and is a kind of preparation for it.

Montaigne summed up much of this wisdom on overcoming the fear of death in his essay 'To philosophize is to learn how to die', pointing out the many different ways in which death can carry us off – one example he gives is that of his own brother, who was struck by a ball just above the right ear whilst playing tennis, and 'five or six hours after . . . died from an apoplexy caused by the blow'– in order to remind us that we can die at pretty much any moment and thus have to prepare ourselves for it.

He offers a number of suggestions. We should, he says, deprive death of its strangeness by thinking about it often, including when we are enjoying ourselves, and he writes approvingly of the ancient Egyptians, who 'in the midst of their banquets and celebrations . . . would bring a skeleton in to serve as a warning to their guests'. He tells us also that we should, like him, when we are reading or chatting to people, find out how different individuals died, in order to model ourselves on those who died well. 'Whoever taught men how to die would teach them how to live', he comments in his typically laconic manner. What Montaigne has in mind is the idea we have already encountered that life itself is deeply bound up with death, in the sense that the whole of life is a progression towards death. '[The] being which you enjoy is a part equally of death and life,' he writes, and forms part of the 'interweaving of things' in nature. Because we are always dying whilst alive, all 'that you live, you rob from life, living at her expense' (*'Que philosopher, c'est apprendre à mourir'*: 131–138). We should see ourselves, Montaigne suggests, as part of the cycle of life and death, and be willing to relinquish gracefully what has only been loaned to us, so to speak. He also suggests that we should try to view our individual lives from the perspective of eternity. Consider, he says, those tiny creatures which live for one day: it makes no difference from our perspective if one such creature dies at eight in the morning or at five in the afternoon and, similarly, from the perspective of infinity it makes no difference if we live a long or short life.

Not everyone will find any or all of these arguments useful in seeking to find consolation in the face of death. But I would certainly recommend reflection on them to see if you might find them of help. Levi, however, as I intimated earlier, rejected the idea that the proper object of philosophical reflection should be death. In his book *If This is a Man*, he speaks of 'the demolition of a man' that went on in Auschwitz: the reduction of human beings to the state or level of animals, as he put it, a procedure that was carried out by depriving the prisoners of all their possessions, stripping them naked, making them defecate and urinate in public, shaving them, and replacing their names with numbers. Levi spoke of this as the destruction of the personality and, amazed at how quickly and easily such destruction can take place, he wrote that

> our personality is fragile, and much more in danger than our life; and the ancient sages, instead of admonishing us to 'remember

that you must die' would have done better
to remind us of this greater danger that
menaces us. (*Se questo è un uomo*: 48)

Montaigne thought that one of the central reasons to fear death was that everyone is subject
to it, whereas other misfortunes are not in this
way inevitable. And he is, of course, right about
that. Given that this is so, we might well side with
Montaigne and seek consolation for our mortality in the kind of way he suggests. But we might
think, otherwise, that Levi's point provides consolation for our mortality precisely because we come
to see that it is not the worst that can befall us,
even if it is inevitable – as the destruction of the
personality, thankfully, is not. We might, that is
to say, be able to face death better if we see that
a worse fate has not afflicted us in our lives, find
gratitude in ourselves to life for that and hence
see death as something to be feared less. At any
rate, Levi's thought, or what I have derived from
it, joins hands here with Montaigne, since the
latter suggests that if we have had a good life we
should seek to be grateful for this and leave life as
we leave a feast – replete and satisfied. And, Montaigne goes on, 'if you have never learned how to
use life, if life is useless to you, what does it matter

Meditating upon death may well take from us some of our fear of it.

to you if you have lost it?' – that is, if you die?
(*Que philosopher, c'est apprendre à mourir*: 139).
If, as Hume suggested, we all have a tendency to
'complain at once of the shortness of life, and of
its vanity and sorrow' – 'such is the greatness of
human misery, it reconciles even contradictions',
he remarks tersely (*Dialogues and Natural History
of Religion*: 100) – then what, in their different
ways, Levi and Montaigne are seeking to do is to
break us of this contradiction by helping us to be
grateful for what we have and for this very reason
better able to let it go when the time comes. The
solution to death is found in how one lives.

Death and the Act of Dying

I have so far not clearly distinguished death
itself, the fact of being dead, from the process or
act of dying – the physical collapse of the body.
But the distinction is important because it is
possible to fear one and not the other. Simone
de Beauvoir, for example, in her book about her
mother's last months, *A Very Easy Death*, reports
at one point the demeanour of both her mater-
nal grandmother and her father in the face of
death. 'My grandmother,' she writes,

was aware that she was dying. She said quite happily: 'I am going to eat a last little boiled egg, and then I shall go to rejoin Gustave.' She had never put much energy into living. At the age of eighty-four, she vegetated morosely: dying did not disturb her. (*Une mort très douce*: 107–8)

And of her father she writes that,

[he] did not show less courage. 'Ask your mother to send no priest. I don't want to play a comedy,' he said to me. And he gave me certain instructions on practical matters. Financially ruined, bitter, he accepted nothingness as serenely as grand-mother accepted paradise. (*Une mort très douce*: 108)

No doubt both of these people had reasons to accept death as they did, reasons to do with the compromised nature of their individual lives. But, of course, everyone's life is compromised in some way and, moreover, de Beauvoir saw them both as courageous. Like Philip Gould, they were not frightened of death, of the state of being dead. So a question we must ask ourselves is whether we are frightened of death itself or only the act of dying. Without being honest with ourselves about that, we cannot, I think, begin to cope with the fear in question. We each have to reflect on this for ourselves.

De Beauvoir's mother, who died of cancer, was frightened of both death and dying. Yet, despite her Catholic faith, she did not seek the aid of a priest during her terrible illness, and she did not pray, something which is to be explained, says de Beauvoir, by the fact that, for her, prayer was 'an exercise that demanded attention and reflection, a certain state of the soul' (*Une mort très douce*: 107), and it would therefore have exhausted her. De Beauvoir continues:

> She knew what she should have said to God: 'Heal me. But thy will be done: I accept death.' But she did not accept it. In this moment of truth, she did not want to utter insincere words. Nonetheless, she did not grant herself the right to rebel. She remained silent: 'God is good.' . . . In any case, Mother feared neither God nor the devil: simply leaving the world. (*Une mort très douce*: 107)

But even she had moments of 'joy' and, at times, was 'at peace with herself', finding, 'on this death bed, a kind of happiness' (*Une mort très douce*: 71). This is not to suggest that she did not suffer terribly. It is simply to insist that, despite that suffering, she found something in the process of dying that was positive. In her case, this was because, says de Beauvoir, for the first time in her life, she really gave herself over, without scruple, to her desires and to pleasure.

None of this is to deny that many die awful, wretched deaths, even in developed, affluent parts of the world with good medical services. But it is to say that, if we are lucky, and if we open ourselves to this possibility, even the process of dying can give us something. I am sure that central to that luck is the love or friendship of others. In death, as I mentioned earlier, we are alone, but the affections of others can do something to mitigate that.

In considering why her mother's faith could not console her for her death, de Beauvoir compares the immortality that religion might offer and that offered by her own fame from being a writer. She says: 'Religion could do no more for my mother than could the hope of post-humous success for me. Whether one imagines it as celestial or terrestrial, immortality does not console one for death if one is attached to life' (*Une mort très douce*: 108). The point here is that immortality as offered by religion is, whatever else it is, not the same as immortality here on earth, and for some religious believers it may precisely be the latter that they want – or, if not immortality, at least more life here below. And of course a non-believer might want that too. Woody Allen made much the same point in his typically droll manner when he remarked: 'I don't want to achieve immortality through my work; I want to achieve immortality through not dying'. And when he was asked if he would like to live on in the hearts of others, he replied: 'I would like to live on in my apartment' (*The Illustrated Woody Allen Reader*: 250; 259).

But it may be a matter of temperament whether one finds consolation after all in the way in which the dead can live on in the hearts of others. One of the things that makes such a thought more difficult for those in the modern age is the way in which death has been stripped of much of its ritual quality and removed to the edges of our lives: death is not a permanent presence for us, as it was for those of previous ages. We have created a world in which death has no place. De Beauvoir brings this out forcefully when she reflects on the things she sees in the shop windows whilst her mother lies dying in a clinic:

> Perfumes, furs, lingerie, jewels: luxurious arrogance of a world where death does not have its place. But it is crouching behind this façade, in the secret greyness of clinics, hospitals, closed rooms. And I no longer know any other truth. (*Une mort très douce*: 92)

We are in denial most of the time about death, which is one of the reasons why those, like Gould, who have written about their own experience of dying stress again and again the importance of being honest with themselves that this is what is happening – that they are dying. Such honesty does not defeat death, but, Gould says, it does provide freedom from it. Ivan too, in Tolstoy's story, only becomes free when he finally acknowledges that he is dying and that there is nothing he can do to change that.

In any case, there *is* a sense in which the dead live on, though I do not mean this in any superstitious or literal way. I know, for example, that my father – what he did and how he lived his life, for good and ill – is often present to me in my thoughts and feelings, and I seek still to learn from the manner in which he lived. In *Thoughts on Happiness*, Alain writes that

> [t]he dead are not dead, which is clear enough, since we live. The dead think, speak and act; they can advise, desire, approve, blame. All that is true. But it is necessary to hear it. All that is in us; all that is really alive in us. (*Propos sur le bonheur*: 143)

As Alain says, visiting the graves of the dead can, if we listen carefully, return us to life, because the dead have much to say to us. And, we may add, there is little doubt that the dead more generally, including those one has never known, can play a large part in one's inner life, in one's thoughts and feelings. Through books, films, photographs, music and so on, they speak to us, if only we listen carefully. In an interview, the writer W. G. Sebald was happy to be called a 'ghost hunter', and his work expresses very finely the attempt to listen carefully to the dead. As he says: 'I have always had at the back of my mind this notion that . . . these people [the dead] aren't really gone, they just hover somewhere at

the perimeter of our lives and keep coming in
on brief visits' ('Ghost Hunter': 39). In his writings, Sebald teaches us how we might listen. As
he says in another interview:

> The attitude for which I strive – and this
> is something that one has to learn – is an
> attitude of mourning. Not in any sentimental sense, but rather the full awareness
> that one is seeing something that is disappearing: a body, a society, a state, a part of
> nature or whatever. ('*Eine Trauerhaltung
> lernen*': 115)

Although, of course, Sebald is speaking here of
more than individual human beings, it is clear
that we can apply what he says more narrowly to
those who are dead. His writings seek, as I have
said, to make us attentive. They do so because
they are infinitely focused, with a kind of grieving love, on the details of individual lives and on
what the people in question made of them. The
fact that Sebald himself died in 2001 adds to
what we can learn from him: he is a ghost speaking of ghosts, a dead writer who speaks of death,
and in this way he invites us to be less frightened of death by drawing us towards seeing our

own death as part of an inevitable cycle of things that has its own melancholy beauty.

As I say, it may be a matter of temperament whether these kinds of reflections can console us in, and for, our own death. But if you find consolation in them, it might be that you can also find such, as Gould suggests, in a sense of community with those already dead. To die is to enter into the realm of those who have already died, as if one were now to join them. At any rate, I find something consoling in that thought. Most of the men and women I admire are dead, and I have the sense that, when I die, I shall join them, not in any literal way, but simply in the sense that then I shall be numbered amongst them. And I am not alone in having some such a sense of things. De Beauvoir, in her account of her mother's illness and death, tells of the funeral. Sitting with her sister in the hearse, she looked at the coffin in which their mother's body was laid. De Beauvoir reports what her sister said and then makes a comment:

'The only thing that consoles me,' she said to me, 'is that I too will go that way. Without that, it would be too unfair!' Yes. We were taking part in the dress rehearsal for our own burial. (*Une mort très douce*: 117)

De Beauvoir's sister's sentiment may not have been exactly the same as my sense of joining the dead, but it certainly expresses a kind of solidarity or community with the dead. It expresses a similar sense of going to join the dead, and clearly her sister thought of this in terms of a kind of justice. I do not know whether that made her better able to confront her own mortality and integrate it more seamlessly into her life, but it certainly opens up such a possibility.

My sense about these things is also this: those men and women I admire, and who have died, have managed to achieve something – precisely, their death. And that gives me a powerful feeling that, if they were able to do this, so can I. I have the sense that it *cannot be as bad as all that* if they have done it. I think here of all the times in my life when I have been frightened by some difficult challenge and, in the end, things turned out to be easier than I had imagined. I am always surprised at how resilient human beings are when things are very difficult. Gould says of his cancer treatment that before it began he thought he would simply be unable to cope with it. But cope with it he did. And then he was told that he would never eat normally, and he got used to that too. 'Then you realise – whatever they throw at you, you can deal with it'. He managed to cope even with his '[e]ndless, endless pain' (*When I Die*: 121; 122). He did not in any sense value his pain, and he wanted it reduced as much as possible, but it did, he says, give him a sense that now, for the first time, he understood what pain was, and therefore could understand the pain of others. To that extent, it clearly opened him to the world.

Changing Attitudes

In the modern bourgeois world we place an enormous emphasis upon the security of the individual. This has no doubt brought many benefits, but it has, along with other things, such as secularization and the advance of medical science, also unquestionably made us much more intolerant of pain than those of previous ages were. It has also made us more fearful of death. In his essay 'On the Fear of Death', William Hazlitt was scathing about this aspect of modern life. Speaking of the tendency to cling to life as such in our modern, civilized world, he comments that in the past people threw themselves

> into all the vicissitudes and dangers of war, or staked their all upon a single die, or some one passion, which if they could not have gratified, life became a burden to them – now our strongest passion is to think, our chief amusement is to read new plays, new poems, new novels, and this we may do at our leisure, in perfect security ... A life of action and danger moderates the dread of death. It not only gives us fortitude to bear pain, but teaches us at every step the precarious tenure on which we hold our present being. ('On the Fear of Death': 479–80)

The complaint is, as J. P. Stern put it when discussing some aspects of the modern condition, that we live in an age of the 'atrophy of the heart and the dulling of the senses[,] in a world where conformism and commerce, the civil service and bourgeois taboos, have taken the place of heroism and adventure' (*Idylls and Realities*: 37). Of course, death was feared in the past, but security was not considered to be of supreme value. Death itself, in the pursuit of some good, could be seen as something deeply worthy. We do not see things this way, not even when we feel that it might be better to die than to live, as in cases of acute and pointless pain. Even when we speak of heroic deaths, as in war or in other acts of courage or valour, we see such death as an exception that confirms our general attitude. We have very little understanding of what Nietzsche called, in a striking phrase, *'der verschwenderische Geist'*, the squandering spirit. Because we place so much emphasis on individual security, we no longer really understand those characters from the past who squandered themselves by living at the limits of their capacities, pushing themselves to the point where they risked destroying themselves, not least because they often risked destroying others in the process. One good example, to which I have already referred, is that given by Antony and Cleopatra in their magnificent egoism. The writings of the Austrian writer Stefan Zweig are replete with examples – indeed, his work is in many ways a kind of lament for the loss of such figures, or their increasingly rare occurrence in the modern world: Magellan, Balzac, Casanova, among others.

Of course, one must not exaggerate, and there are modern exceptions, in the arts or sport, but even here the bureaucratization of existence has made such inroads that these areas of life have become massively over-professionalized and regulated. It would be a romantic fantasy to suppose that we could go back to living as earlier ages did. Nonetheless, in Nietzsche's idea of the squandering spirit there is a lesson in how to think productively about death, and with less fear. For it is open to us to see our lives much more in terms of a kind of venture or quest than we often do. Focused on making our external lives as secure as possible, we forget that we can make our inner lives a scene of the most extraordinary adventure, and that we can challenge ourselves much more than we suppose we can. Our inner lives can be much more like the kind Hazlitt imagined, lives of action and danger. We effectively smother such a possibility by our relentless desire for happiness and our deep incapacity to accept suffering – melancholy, disappointment, loss and so on – as completely and utterly normal, by our secret – and sometimes not so secret – suspicion, or fantasy, that these things have no real place in the world. A quite different possibility, more in line with Hazlitt's view, is well articulated by the opening passage of Hermann Hesse's novel *Gertrude*:

When I look back across my life from the outside, it does not seem especially happy. Nonetheless, I can with even less justice call it unhappy, despite all the errors. It is in the end also quite foolish to ask about happiness and unhappiness, for it seems to me that I would give up the unhappiest days of my life with more difficulty than all the cheerful ones. If in a human life the task is to accept the inevitable clear-sightedly, to suffer good and evil fully, and to conquer an inner, more authentic, non-contingent destiny next to one's external destiny, then my life has been neither poor nor bad. If my external destiny has passed over me as over all other people, inevitably and as decreed by the gods, nonetheless my inner destiny has been my own work, whose sweetness or bitter-ness is mine, and for which I consider that I alone should accept the responsibility. (*Gertrud*: 7)

We are back to the sense of the immanence of death in life. For, if you manage to see your life in the way Hesse expresses, you might be able to see your death not as something dreadful that stands at the end of your life, but rather as something that you have earned, worked for, something that is worthy of you. Whether it arrives suddenly or slowly, your death could be something that you make fully your own because you see it as being at one with your life, as being something that you *live* each day, just as you make yours the rest of what happens to you by carving out of it an inner destiny parallel to your external destiny. To that extent, as I suggested earlier, the fact that we are mortal is central to the meaning we can find in life.

Wittgenstein recommended to his pupils that they 'go the bloody hard way', by which he meant that philosophy should never be a mere intellectual or academic pursuit but should be bound up with one's *whole* being, so that it helps one see what one *really thinks* and not simply what one *thinks one thinks* because it is convenient or fashionable or impressive or useful for career purposes. I am suggesting that there is something in what Wittgenstein says for life more generally. What matters is much less the length of your life than the spirit in which you live it. The struggle to live in a spirit of integrity is also a struggle to see one's mortality for what it is, to *live* one's mortality, precisely because it is inevitable and, as part of our external destiny, needs to be made one's own in the inner life.

This is the deepest lesson that Tolstoy's Ivan Ilyich has to teach us: his living a lie was his living without integrity, without really making anything *his own*, and it was precisely for this reason that he was so terrified of death. Being an individual is not so much a matter of doing what others have not done or do not do, as it is a matter of doing it in a spirit expressive of your whole being. If you do this, then, as Gould says, you do not beat death; but death cannot beat you.

Some Final Thoughts

I have tried in this book to offer some productive ways to think about adversity in four different contexts. In these few final comments I should like to draw out and make explicit one or two general points that I see running through the discussions. In doing so, I offer a couple of further suggestions for thinking about adversity.

Scepticism

It is important, I think, if you want to make sense of the adversity in your life to seek to be sceptical. This means a number of things. In part it is a matter of acknowledging that there are many things you do not know – far more than you do know – about the human condition. Life is deeply mysterious, and the motives that human beings have for doing what they do are often deeply obscure to everyone, including the individual concerned. Do not fight this mystery; seek to *live* it. Try to give others, and yourself, the benefit of the doubt. Judge, if at all, coolly and after reflection.

Being sceptical is also a matter of your relation to what you do believe. You can hold your opinions in a kind of tentative fashion. The truth is that the position we tend to adopt automatically when we have an opinion is that we *know*. Hence the Franco-Romanian philosopher E. M. Cioran said in his book *A Short History of Decay* that 'man is the dogmatic being par excellence' (*Précis de décomposition*: 88). The advantage of being sceptical is that it helps to undercut adversity, both in oneself and with others. As Cioran points out, history is a scene of such relentless suffering inflicted by human beings on themselves and on each other because – or, at any rate, largely because – there have been endless individuals who were sure they knew the truth and sought to get others to agree with them. For those who feel sure they have the answers are usually pretty keen to impose them on others. I would add to this the point I made in the Introduction, that human beings are ontological misfits: the claim that one knows the truth is invariably an attempt to conceal from oneself one's ontological insecurity, by making it seem that one has the stability of truth – that one is not insecure after all. If we were at home in the world we would not experience or create adversity as we do.

And it is not only at the large, historical level that scepticism might be helpful. In interpersonal relationships scepticism helps to reduce adversity, because it means that one is much more willing to be open to the other's point of view. It can help also with the attainment of individual inner peace, since it encourages a kind of cheerful tolerance in the face of disagreement.

Of course, it is immensely hard to put such scepticism into practice. But if you can mobilize it in yourself, even only occasionally or haltingly, you will have done much to reduce the incidence of adversity in your life.

Weakness

So do not *fight* your vulnerability, your weakness. Meditate on it and seek to incorporate it consciously in your life. Ancient thinkers such as Marcus Aurelius and Seneca recommended that, in order to cope with life's adversities, we should practise for them in advance, through thought experiments. The key is to acknowledge that bad things will happen to you because that is just the way life is, and to meditate on them, so that if and when they arrive you will be able to cope better. Hence Seneca writes:

> For by looking ahead to all [the bad] that may happen as though it were going to happen, [you] . . . will soften the attacks of all ills, which bring nothing unforeseen to those who are prepared and expectant, but come as a serious blow to those who . . . expect only blessings. ('On the Tranquillity of the Mind': 130)

Imagine yourself in various situations of adversity and ask yourself how you could most constructively react in them, to them. If you do this, you will have a good chance of coming somewhat more prepared to them and may make less of a mess of them than you otherwise would, because you will have acknowledged your weakness from the first. I also find it helpful sometimes to imagine that a wise and generous but rigorous person is accompanying me through the day. Montaigne is my favourite, because he is so phenomenally well-balanced. And when I am about to get angry or frustrated, I imagine what he would say to me, and I invariably find that this helps to put my feelings into perspective and allows me to get a grip on them and remain calmer. Thinking, too, about how self-indulgent it is to get worked up about some small issue, as I sometimes do, in a world 'bursting with sin and sorrow', as Johnson put it, and in which I have been spared the worst forms of suffering that have taken place and are taking place right now, also helps, I find.

Pleasure

The other side of the coin is this: cope with adversity by seeking out those things in life that give you pleasure and a sense of peace. Seneca advises us to go for walks, to drink wine, and in general to show kindness to ourselves – for it is surprising how hard it often is to be kind to oneself. Montaigne too advises this. Nietzsche as well, who tells us we should think each morning of something pleasant we can do during the day, not least to help us deal successfully with any adversity we may encounter. It is important to be rigorously realistic with oneself, but it is also important to find good things in life. And

Montaigne suggests, in his essay 'On diversion', that, if we are assailed by painful or difficult thoughts, we should divert the mind:

> [S]ome distressing idea gets hold of me; I find it quicker to change it than to subdue it. If I cannot replace it with an opposite one, I find at least a different one. Change is always a solace, dissolves the idea and dispels it. If I cannot fight it, I flee it. (*De la diversion*': 51)

One can do this for others too. Montaigne tells us that he once had to console a lady who was feeling distressed. Instead of seeking to show her that her distress was not justified and directly confronting her suffering, he spoke to her about her feelings and then gradually took the conversation away to other things. And, he says, 'I kept her composed and totally calm as long as I was there' ('*De la diversion*': 47).

Urbanity

I think we might sum up these thoughts by invoking the notion of urbanity. For to be urbane

is, in one of its aspects, to be able to laugh ironically and good-heartedly at human foolishness,
including one's own. Seneca makes this point
when he reminds us that we all get moments
in which we are filled with hatred or disgust for
the human race. Or, as G. K. Chesterton has it:
'Every man has hated humanity . . . Every man
has had humanity in his nostrils like a suffocat-
ing smell' (*Heretics*: 185). And Seneca's advice is
that we should, when in this mood, try to find
human beings not hateful but ludicrous.

Another way to express this would be to
remind ourselves of the wonderful comment by
Chremes, a character in *The Self-Tormentor*, one
of the plays of the Roman playwright Terence – it
was actually one of the classical quotations that
Montaigne had inscribed on a beam in his study:
'I am a human being and I consider nothing
human alien to me'.

Running through this book have been two
key ideas. Firstly, I have wanted to bring out
the way in which forms of adversity – ambivalence, incomprehension, vulnerability and
dissolution – are *also* things for which we can
be grateful. We could not become adults without
experiencing feelings of ambivalence, so they
are to be welcomed on that account; we would

not find anyone erotically appealing if we fully understood him or her, and to that extent incomprehension is valuable; we could not enjoy the delights of the body, unless we could also fall ill, and so we have reason to cherish our vulnerability; and we would find little or no meaning in our lives if we were immortal, and so our dissolution, the process of dying that is with us all our lives and finally ends in our death, is not wholly an unwelcome intruder into our lives. As Hume writes:

> Good and ill are universally intermingled and confounded; happiness and misery, wisdom and folly, virtue and vice. Nothing is purely and entirely of a piece. All advantages are attended with disadvantages. An universal compensation prevails in all conditions of being and existence. And it is not possible for us, by our most chimerical wishes, to form the idea of a station or situation altogether desirable. (*Dialogues and Natural History of Religion*: 183)

Adversity is inevitable. We must accept that, and not fight or regret it all the time. We should also remember that it can bring good things.

The second key idea in this book, related to the first, is that not despite but on account of all the mistakes you have made in your life, and not despite but because of all the forms of adversity that you have experienced and had to cope with, have confronted well or made a mess of, the life you have lived and are living has given you a unique insight into your condition and the human condition more generally. The adversity in your life has been a precious source of enlightenment. You will face more adversity. As you do, you should seek not simply to cope with it as constructively as possible, turning it to account, but also remember that it is giving you an understanding of things that is irreplaceably valuable. It is part of your inheritance as a human being – and you should seek not to consider it alien to you.

Homework

In addition to the books I have discussed in the main body of the text, and amongst the many things that could be studied with profit, I would recommend the following relevant works.

Introduction

Pierre Hadot's *Philosophy as a Way of Life: Spiritual Exercises from Socrates to Foucault* (Malden, MA: Wiley-Blackwell, 1995), tr. Michael Chase, ed. and intro. Arnold Davidson, provides both an introduction to philosophy and makes a case for the therapeutic value of philosophical reflection.

1. Ambivalence; or, Adversity in the Family

Julia Blackburn's *The Three of Us* (London: Jonathan Cape, 2008) provides many insights into the nature of a deeply fractured family from the point of view of the child. A painful but fascinating read.

A useful introduction to Melanie Klein's thinking, with references, is Hanna Segal's *Melanie Klein* (New York: Viking Press, 1979).

Yasujiro Ozu's film *Tokyo Story* (1953) is a mercilessly insightful dissection of relations between parents and children.

2. Incomprehension; or, Adversity in Love

Simon May's *Love: a History* (New Haven: Yale University Press, 2012) provides a good survey of some of the varying attitudes towards love in the Western tradition.

Philosophies of Love (Lanham: Rowman and Littlefield Publishers, 1971), eds David L. Norton and Mary F. Kille, is a really useful anthology, containing extracts from key philosophers on the different kinds of love.

Irving Singer has written extensively on love

from a philosophical point of view. His *Philosophy of Love: a Partial Summing-Up* (Cambridge, MA: MIT Press, 2009) is a good place to start.

Five interesting case studies from psychoanalysis exploring some of the difficulties of intimate relations are to be found in Deborah Luepnitz's *Schopenhauer's Porcupines: Intimacy and its Dilemmas* (New York: Basic Books, 2002).

C. S. Lewis's *The Four Loves* (London: HarperCollins, 2012) has some stimulating things to say about different kinds of love. His idea that one of the functions of eros is to play the buffoon in our lives has the ring of truth about it.

Jonathan Lear's *Love and its Place in Nature* (New Haven: Yale University Press, 1998) explores its theme from a psychoanalytic point of view.

Love, Sex and Tragedy: How the Ancient World Shapes Our Lives (London: John Murray, 2004) by Simon Goldhill is a thoroughly enjoyable read which relates the modern and ancient worlds in order to enlighten us about our condition.

Caroline J. Simon's *The Disciplined Heart* (Grand Rapids, Michigan: William B. Eerdmans, 1997) discusses love in various contexts from a philosophical and theological point of view, helpfully exploring many literary examples.

Amongst filmmakers, I would especially recommend the work of Michelangelo Antonioni as a director who explores insightfully problems of erotic love in modernity. His *L'Avventura* (1960) is a masterpiece. Pretty much most of Eric Rohmer's films deal with the same issue, in a quite different way. His early *Ma nuit chez Maud* (1969) is still as pertinent now as when it was made. And Woody Allen has much to say on modern love that is helpful. My favourite is probably *Hannah and her Sisters* (1986).

3. Vulnerability; or, Adversity in the Body

Sarah Bakewell's *How to Live: a Life of Montaigne in One Question and Twenty Attempts at an Answer* (London: Vintage, 2011) is very helpful on many aspects of Montaigne's philosophy, including his attitude to death and illness. Michael Screech's *Montaigne and Melancholy* (Harmondsworth: Penguin, 1991) is fascinating on Montaigne's ideas, his intellectual context and background, and is full of wise things.

A really helpful book on Kafka's attitude to his body and to his illness is Sander Gilman's *Franz Kafka, the Jewish Patient* (London: Routledge, 1995).

Virginia Woolf's *On Being Ill* (Ashfield, MA: Paris Press, 2002) is the best short piece on illness I know.

4. Dissolution; or, Adversity in Dying

A very helpful reader, which contains a good introductory essay and then extracts from key philosophers on death, is Herbert Fingarette's *Death: Philosophical Soundings* (Chicago: Open Court, 1997).

Death (Stocksfield: Acumen, 2006) by Geoffrey Scarre is one of the better one-volume, concise introductions to the topic of death as discussed in academic philosophy.

Two modern classics on death from the philosophical literature are Bernard Williams's 'The Makropulos Case: Reflections on the Tedium of Immortality' in his *Problems of the Self* (Cambridge: Cambridge University Press, 1976) and Thomas Nagel's (partial) rejoinder 'Death' in his *Mortal Questions* (Cambridge: Cambridge University Press, 2012).

Hirokazu Kore-Eda's film *After Life* (1998) is an insightful exploration of death.

Bibliography

The quotations used in this book are drawn from the following sources. The quotations in translation are mine, except where indicated in the body text, and I have provided details of the most readily accessible English translation, where available.

Alain (Émile-Auguste Chartier), *Propos sur le bonheur* (Paris: Gallimard, 2009)

Allen, Woody, *The Illustrated Woody Allen Reader*, ed. Linda Sunshine (London: Jonathan Cape, 1993)

Arendt, Hannah, 'On Humanity in Dark Times: Thoughts About Lessing' in *Men in Dark Times* (San Diego: Harcourt, 1967)

Aristotle, *Nicomachean Ethics*, tr. Terence Irwin (Indianapolis: Hacket, 1999)

Bate, Walter Jackson, *Samuel Johnson* (London: Hogarth Press, 1978)

Blecher, Max, *Scarred Hearts*, tr. Henry Howard, intro. Paul Bailey (London: Old Street Publishing, 2008)

Bloom, Allan, *Love and Friendship* (New York: Simon & Schuster, 1993)

Boswell, James and Johnson, Samuel, *The Table-Talk of Samuel Johnson* (Ulan Press, 2012)

Camus, Albert, *La Peste*, ed. W. J. Strachan (London: Methuen, 1965)

Chesterton, G. K., *Heretics* (London: Bodley Head, 1905)

Cioran, E. M., *Précis de decomposition* (Paris: Gallimard, 2011)

Cousins, Norman, *Anatomy of an Illness* (New York: W. W. Norton and Company, 2005)

De Beauvoir, Simone, *Une mort très douce* (Paris: Gallimard, 2011)

Eliot, George, *Middlemarch*, ed. W. J. Harvey (Harmondsworth: Penguin, 1985)

Eliot, T. S., *The Cocktail Party* (London: Faber & Faber, 1982)

Frank, Arthur, *The Wounded Storyteller: Body, Illness, and Ethics* (Chicago: University of Chicago Press, 1997)

Freud, Sigmund, 'Der Familienroman der Neurotiker' in vol. VII of *Gesammelte Werke*, eds Anna Freud, Marie Bonaparte, E. Bibring, W. Hoffer, E. Kris and O. Osakower (Frankfurt am Main: Fischer Verlag, 1999)

Gosse, Edmund, *Father and Son*, intro. Michael

Newton (Oxford: Oxford University Press, 2004)

Gould, Philip, *When I Die: Lessons from the Death Zone*, ed. Keith Blackmore (London: Abacus, 2013)

Hazlitt, William, 'On the Fear of Death', in *Selected Writings*, ed. Ronald Blythe (Harmondsworth: Penguin, 1970)

Hesse, Hermann, *Gertrud* (Frankfurt: Suhrkamp Verlag, 2006)

Hume, David, *Dialogues and Natural History of Religion*, ed. and notes J. C. A. Gaskin (Oxford: Oxford University Press, 1993)

Johnson, Samuel, *The History of Rasselas, Prince of Abissinia*, ed. and intro. D. J. Enright (Harmondsworth: Penguin, 1985)

Josipovici, Gabriel, *Contre-Jour* (Manchester: Carcanet, 1986)

Kafka, Franz, *Brief an den Vater* (Frankfurt am Main: Fischer Verlag, 2003)

Kafka, Franz, *The Diaries of Franz Kafka 1910–1923*, tr. Joseph Kresch and Martin Greenberg, with the cooperation of Hannah Arendt, ed. Max Brod (Harmondsworth: Penguin, 1972)

Kafka, Franz, *Letters to Felice*, tr. James Stern and Elizabeth Duckworth, eds Erich Heller and Jürgen Born (Harmondsworth: Penguin, 1978)

Lampedusa, Tomasi di, *Il Gattopardo*, ed. Gioacchino Lanza Tomasi (Milano: Feltrinelli, 2011)

Levi, Primo, *Se questo è un uomo*, afterword Cesare Segre (Turin: Einaudi, 2013)

Levi, Primo, *Il sistema periodico* (Turin: Einaudi, 2012)

Márai, Sándor, *Embers*, tr. Carol Brown Janeway (Harmondsworth: Penguin, 2003)

Montaigne, M. de, *Essais: Livres 1–3*, biographical background and intro. Alexandre Micha. *'Que philosopher, c'est apprendre à mourir'* is in volume 1; *'De la diversion'* and *'De l'experience'* are in volume 3 (Paris: Flammarion, 1969)

Murdoch, Iris, *The Sovereignty of Good* (London: Ark, 1970)

Nietzsche, F., *Menschliches, Allzumenschliches: ein Buch für freie Geister*. Volume II of *Sämtliche Werke: Kritische Studienausgabe in 15 Einzelbänden*, ed. Giorgio Colli and Mazzino Montinari (Berlin: Walter de Gruyter, 1980)

Plutarch, 'On the Avoidance of Anger' in *Essays*, tr. Robin Waterfield, intro. and annotation Ian Kidd (Harmondsworth: Penguin, 1992)

Proust, Marcel, *À la recherche du temps perdu I: Du côté de chez Swann* (Paris: Gallimard, 2009), intro. and notes Antoine Compagnon

Rilke, R. M., *Briefe an einen jungen Dichter/Briefe*

an eine junge Frau, foreword Joachim W. Storck (Zürich: Diogenes Verlag, 2006)

Rochefoucauld, F. de la, *Maximes*, biographical background, intro., ed., notes and variants, index Jacques Truchet (Paris: Flammarion, 1977)

Rowe, Dorothy, *Depression: the Way out of Your Prison* (London: Routledge, 2003)

Sartre, Jean-Paul, *The War Diaries: November 1939–March 1940*, tr. Quintin Hoare (New York: Pantheon Books, 1984)

Sebald, W. G., 'Ghost Hunter' in *The Emergence of Memory*, ed. Lynne Sharon Schwartz (New York: Seven Stories Press, 2007)

Sebald, W. G., 'Eine Trauerhaltung lernen' in *'Auf ungeheuer dünnem Eis': Gespräche 1971 bis 2001*, ed. Torsten Hoffmann (Frankfurt am Main: Fischer Verlag, 2011)

Seneca, 'On Anger' and 'On the Tranquillity of the Mind' in *Dialogues and Essays*, tr. John Davie, intro. and notes Tobias Reinhardt (Oxford: Oxford University Press, 2008)

Sontag, Susan, *Illness as Metaphor and AIDS and its Metaphors* (Harmondsworth: Penguin, 2002)

Stendhal, *De l'amour*, biographical background and preface Michel Crouzet (Paris: Flammarion, 2011)

Stern, J. P., *Idylls and Realities* (London: Methuen, 1971)

Svevo, Italo, *La coscienza di Zeno*, ed. Cristina Benussi, intro. Franco Marcoaldi (Milan: Feltrinelli, 2011)

Tolstoy, Leo, *Anna Karenina*, tr. Louise and Aylmer Maude, intro. and notes W. Gareth Jones (Oxford: Oxford University Press, 2008)

Tolstoy, Leo, *The Death of Ivan Ilyich and Other Stories*, tr. Ronald Wilks, Anthony Briggs, David McDuff, intro. Anthony Briggs (Harmondsworth: Penguin, 2008)

Updike, John, 'At War with My Skin' in *Self-Consciousness* (New York: Random House, 1989)

Weiss, Peter, *Abschied von den Eltern* (Frankfurt am Main: Suhrkamp Verlag, 1964)

Wittgenstein, Ludwig, *Tractatus Logico-Philosophicus*, tr. D. F. Pears and B. F. McGuinness (London: Routledge, 1975)

Wollheim, Richard, *The Thread of Life* (Cambridge: Cambridge University Press, 1986)

Translations into English of foreign language texts listed above (where available)

Camus, Albert, *The Plague*, tr. Robin Buss, intro. Tony Judt (Harmondsworth: Penguin, 2002)

Cioran, E. M., *A Short History of Decay*, tr. Richard Howard (New York: Arcade, 1998)

De Beauvoir, Simone, *A Very Easy Death*, tr. Patrick O'Brien (New York: Pantheon Books, 1999)

Freud, Sigmund, 'Family Romances' in *The Uncanny*, tr. David McLintock, intro. Hugh Haughton (Harmondsworth: Penguin, 2003)

Kafka, Franz, *Dearest Father*, tr. Hannah Turner Stokes and Richard Stokes (Richmond: Oneworld Classics, 2008)

Hesse, Hermann, *Gertrude*, tr. Adele Lewisohn, intro. Thomas Fasano (Claremont: Coyote Canyon Press, 2012)

Lampedusa, Tomasi di, *The Leopard*, tr. Archibald Colquhoun, foreword and appendix Gioacchino Lanza Tomasi, foreword and appendix tr. Guido Waldman (London: Vintage Books, 2007)

Levi, Primo, *If This is a Man/The Truce*, tr. Stuart Woolf (London: Abacus, 1991)

Levi, Primo, *The Periodic Table*, tr. Raymond Rosenthal (Harmondsworth: Penguin, 2000)

Montaigne, M. de, *The Complete Essays*, tr. M. A. Screech (Harmondsworth: Penguin, 1991)

Nietzsche, F., *Human, all too Human: a Book for Free Spirits*, tr. R. J. Hollingdale (Cambridge: Cambridge University Press, 1996)

Proust, Marcel, *In Search of Lost Time I: The Way by Swann's*, tr., intro. and notes Lydia Davis (Harmondsworth: Penguin, 2002)

Rilke, R. M., *Letters to a Young Poet*, tr. Charlie Louth (Harmondsworth: Penguin, 2012)

Rochefoucauld, F. de la, *Maxims*, tr. L. W. Tancock (Harmondsworth: Penguin, 1959)

Stendhal, *Love*, tr. Gilbert Sale and Suzanne Sale, intro. Jean Stewart and B. C. J. G. Knight (Harmondsworth: Penguin, 2004)

Svevo, Italo, *Zeno's Conscience*, tr. and intro. William Weaver (Harmondsworth: Penguin, 2002)

Weiss, Peter, *Leavetaking*, tr. Christopher Levenson (New York: Melville House Publishing, 2014)

Internet

Gould, Philip and Steirn, Adrian, *When I Die: Lessons from the Death Zone*: http://www.youtube.com/watch?v=S2eUwoCUuMc (last accessed 22.8.13)

Acknowledgements

I am very grateful to the following people for their direct and indirect help in my writing of this book: Cindy Chan, Sebastian Gardner, Ryoichi Hirai, Juliette Mitchell, Michael Newton and Edith Steffen. I thank Alain de Botton for inviting me to write it in the first place.

I am especially grateful to Nelly Mars for many conversations in which she explored with me the ideas this book contains, for reading the chapters as they were written, and for providing many suggestions for improvement.

About the Author

DR. CHRISTOPHER HAMILTON is Senior Lecturer in the Philosophy of Religion at King's College London. He is the author of *Middle Age*, part of the Art of Living series published by Acumen Books, and *Living Philosophy*, published by Edinburgh University Press.

Photographic Credits

Explore All of the "Maintenance Manuals for the Mind" from the School of Life Library

How to Think More About Sex
Alain de Botton

ISBN 978-1-250-03065-8 / E-ISBN 978-1-250-03066-5
www.picadorusa.com/
howtothinkmoreaboutsex

How to Stay Sane
Philippa Perry

ISBN 978-1-250-03063-4 / E-ISBN 978-1-250-03064-1
www.picadorusa.com/
howtostaysane

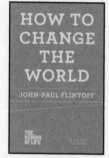

How to Find Fulfilling Work
Roman Krznaric

ISBN 978-1-250-03069-6 / E-ISBN 978-1-250-03070-2
www.picadorusa.com/
howtofindfulfillingwork

How to Change the World
John-Paul Flintoff

ISBN 978-1-250-03067-2 / E-ISBN 978-1-250-03068-9
www.picadorusa.com/
howtochangetheworld

PICADOR

www.picadorusa.com

Available wherever books and e-books are sold.

Explore All of the "Maintenance Manuals for
the Mind" from the School of Life Library

How to Be Alone
Sara Maitland

ISBN 978-1-250-05902-4 / E-ISBN 978-1-250-05903-1
www.picadorusa.com/
howtobealone-maitland

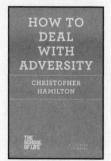

How to Deal with Adversity
Christopher Hamilton

ISBN 978-1-250-05900-0 / E-ISBN 978-1-250-05901-7
www.picadorusa.com/
howtodealwithadversity

How to Think About Exercise
Damon Young

ISBN 978-1-250-05904-8 / E-ISBN 978-1-250-05905-5
www.picadorusa.com/
howtothinkaboutexercise

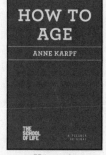

How to Age
Anne Karpf

ISBN 978-1-250-05898-0 / E-ISBN 978-1-250-05899-7
www.picadorusa.com/
howtoage

PICADOR

www.picadorusa.com

Available wherever books and e-books are sold.